Procrastination

The Ultimate Guide to Beat Procrastination, Overcome Laziness, Change Bad Habits and Increase Your Productivity

By

Marcus Holiday

Table of Contents

Introduction

Procrastination is something we may not always admit that we do, but everyone procrastinates in their daily lives, to a certain extent. The reality is, every person has procrastinated at least once in their life. A study on procrastination has revealed that over 90% of the human population procrastinates. While this may offer a little solace to people who often procrastinate, as they now know that they're not alone, it is important that they know how much it gets in their way and inhibits them.

It's a fact—everyone procrastinates or has at least procrastinated before. What's important to understand is that procrastination is inevitable, but there are ways that it can be best managed. We can strive through distractions and mindlessness and still achieve our goals, but with procrastination, it's more difficult. The more you procrastinate, the more you push your goals away. Basically, procrastination means rescheduling your priorities or goals over and over again. It makes you less productive and focused. If you keep procrastinating for a long time, you end up chasing shadows, and your goals will not be reached.

People get up every day with a plan to reach their goals and avoid procrastination, but just as they are about to begin whatever they are working on, procrastination kicks in. One minute, they're making significant progress; the next, they fret and begin putting tasks away to continue them later. At first, it seems like a healthy way out until they realize it has become a pattern in the following couple of days. And what do they get for all their troubles? It's nothing but a huge load of pending tasks. They are then entangled in an unending cycle that inhibits their productivity and progress.

However, an important point to note is that putting away tasks doesn't necessarily relate to laziness. Procrastination and laziness are two different issues that are distinct in their own ways. Laziness pertains to the unwillingness to work or make efforts. Procrastination, on the other hand, is the process of making something less important a priority over things that are more important and tasking. Basically, procrastination is reordering your priorities from the most pleasurable task to the least and undertaking the former first. The former usually involves petty tasks that are less important but easily done, while the latter includes more important and demanding tasks.

Therefore, contrary to popular belief, procrastination is, indeed, a process of the activity. However, as much as procrastination fools you into believing all tasks are equal and can be equally prioritized, it has serious after-effects. If you start your daily schedule with the little tasks and leave the harder ones for last, you will likely end up lacking the will and focus to later do the harder tasks because you would be tired and exhausted. This would cause you to schedule the tasks for a later time. The more this process keeps repeating itself, the more your schedules get clogged with tasks from previous days. Aside from the feeling of shame or guilt that you will probably feel, your productivity level will likely reduce, and the majority of your goals will not be achieved.

Procrastination over the long-term not only could weaken your morale but could also ruin your focus. You suddenly won't see the need for urgency in approaching your goals because you start to believe that doing something, regardless of how small or unimportant, is better than doing nothing at all. According to studies, procrastination stems from cognition. They claim that our brains are wired to inhibit us from doing tasks that we are afraid of or unwilling to do. This explains why we sometimes lose focus when it comes to certain tasks. It is not because the brain doesn't want to make an effort but because it wants to do more enjoyable, comfortable, and problem-free tasks that it is immediately rewarded for.

What this means is that procrastination is as much a choice as it is a cognitive instinct. Over time, it grows into a pattern of decisions, actions, and choices—and it becomes natural behavior. This happens because you made a choice to postpone the important tasks to a later time constantly, and your brain learns to encourage it. Eventually, it becomes a regular behavioral pattern that you can't do without, and slowly but surely, your focus dwindles, and so does your productivity.

Chapter 1: Why Do We Procrastinate?

It's not enough to know that we procrastinate—we need to understand *why* we do this because with the realization comes the power to alter this negative attitude to work and embrace a more positive approach.

As humans, there is a cause for every action we take. Therefore, procrastination is triggered by causes, which produce after-effects that plague us every time we procrastinate. The trigger could be a decision, an action, a choice, etc. Sadly, we aren't all able to identify our personal triggers. This is why we find it difficult to curb or manage our tendency to procrastinate. As I earlier said, we're cognitively wired to be drawn to smaller, more enjoyable, and less tasking things. This is due to our fear of tasks that might prove to be discomforting or have an uncertain end. Therefore, we tend to be inclined to tasks that guarantee a particular level of certainty and comfort, even if it's generally distracting.

Basically, the reason we would rather procrastinate is due to our fears. These fears are the reason why a task doesn't seem appealing or appears too difficult. The task in itself might not be all that difficult, but our fears magnify and make us imagine that it is harder than it is. Consequently, when we are facing and conquering these tasks, we give in to our fears instead and neglect important tasks. Our minds further help with this by simply focusing on other, less important tasks in order to forget about the important ones. This accounts for why we get panic attacks when we remember undone tasks when we think it's all over. Later, I will discuss how you can change your outlook in order to be more productive.

Let's consider an example here. Olga is a writer. To meet her deadlines, she needs to write at least 500 words per hour. In each hour, she dedicates half an hour to meet her word count and the other half-hour to take a break. During her break, she watches movies and stops writing until the next hour strikes. But like all humans, Olga doesn't follow this timing religiously. Sometimes, when the movie is too thrilling, she takes an extra five to ten minutes when a new hour begins.

We are all like Olga. We know our schedule and when we need to do certain tasks, but the urge to remain comfortable and at ease is strong. And even when we manage to ignore this urge to procrastinate, it becomes a struggle to stay focused. Our minds become so frenzied with the distraction to do something less tasking that it is impossible to think correctly. Hence, it becomes a battle with our minds not to switch to a more comfortable and pleasurable task if given the slightest chance.

To overcome a problem, you must know the issues that trigger it. Procrastination is triggered by many factors—one of which is fear. Our minds fear the outcome of things and the morality of doing them, so we end up not doing those things even though we know we should. And sometimes, we can't decide if our fears are worth facing. It is this indecision that makes us procrastinate. We promise ourselves to handle the tasks in a better frame of mind, but we know deep down it's just an excuse to shove it in the back of our minds. Thus, we put it off.

Since fears have been highlighted as one of the primary reasons people procrastinate, it's important to discuss the other different factors that trigger procrastination and how they affect focus and productivity. Although these fears come in various forms, extrinsic and intrinsic, only a few major ones will be discussed in this chapter, and they include:

Fear

Fear, as abstract as it may seem, can arguably be labeled the primary cause of procrastination. Everyone has their individual fears, which, to a certain degree, determines our approach to some things. Fear seems to be able to control and direct the lives of people, and they feel powerless against it.

Fear constitutes a part of our life, which is sometimes beyond our control. Our inability to control it is why it causes us pain and discomfort. What we don't realize is that every part of ourselves, even fear, is subject to us and can be controlled.

In regards to procrastination, there are a number of individual fears we hold, which can make us procrastinate. Some of the fears are:

Fear of Failure

This is arguably the most common type of fear. People fear their tendency to fail more than their will to succeed. This is why people consider an endeavor profitable only if it has a lower risk of failure.

But just because it involves the fear of a negation phenomenon, it doesn't necessarily mean it's the right type of fear. Actually, it is quite the opposite, as the fear of failure leads to a struggle in people. This fear includes your insecurities, and it makes you a prisoner to your emotions. In essence, it shifts your focus from your goals to possible inhibitions that may stand in your way. Therefore, rather than approaching your goal and tackling each inhibition one at a time as it occurs, you instead try to solve them before beginning to chase your goals.

You become so scared of messing up and looking bad, and this fear can be attributed to perfectionism born from your insecurities. Your emotions kick in and suck you deeper into a perpetual cycle of procrastination. You become panic-stricken by the smallest thing that seems out of place and respond negatively to changes. And when everything seems beyond your control, a feeling of inadequacy sets in. Suddenly, the standards you set seem a little out of reach, and you begin to feel like you are unable to meet them. This leads to a struggle inside you on whether you aimed too high or didn't do something properly.

Then, when you approach your goals, you begin to hesitate and apply unnecessary caution. This makes you inactive most of the time because rather than being productive, you're too caught up avoiding errors. Eventually, this inactivity results in you being a perfectionist, making you dwell longer than you should on tasks.

Fear of Success

This is the second most common type of fear that makes us procrastinate. It may seem a little strange, but some people are afraid of success. But this isn't totally without reason. People tend to have this fear because they are afraid of the changes that success would bring to their lives. In some cases, these people have no desire to change and are rigid in their reaction to change. As a result, they tend to put off the tasks that would result in these changes. In other instances, it may be because of the uncertainty surrounding how they would be treated once they succeed. In this case, these people do not feel ready for the limelight and would do anything to put off the unknown for as long as possible.

This fear of change associated with success causes these people to lead lifestyles that are unhealthy to their focus and overall productivity. Apart from having a higher tendency to put inhibitions in their courses, people with this fear would rather indulge themselves in petty activities and tasks that might not even be relevant to their goals. This way, they are able to slow down or possibly avoid any progress towards their chosen goals because they feel that once they succeed, they would have to face even tougher challenges.

Fear of Uncertainty

This fear forms a part of our lives that we are reluctant to deal with. Sometimes, we plunge into an internal struggle when we imagine how things will turn out. We fear that things don't turn out as we expect. As little as this fear might seem, it's detrimental to our focus and productivity.

Basically, being afraid of the uncertain is fear of the future. No one can predict the future, so it remains vastly unknown. Yet, we still sometimes get worked up over something we have no control over. The fear of uncertainty, however, doesn't work independently. It is wired internally to other fears you might have. It can even be said that it's the factor that prompts the other fears. In fact, this is true to a large degree because the outcome of failure or success in achieving your goals is a future possibility. You begin worrying about this outcome, being fearful of how it will turn up even when you have the power to bring up either of them. Instead, you choose to procrastinate.

Being afraid of the uncertain holds you back from venturing out. You end up being so cautious of the steps that lead to success that you miss out on taking them. Not only does this fear render you inactive, but you also become indecisive. You become unsure of taking action because you don't know what to expect — success or failure. In this vein, rather than worrying about the outcomes of your actions, you resort to distractions. Your distractions serve as a means of avoiding the important tasks which would make you progress towards success.

Due to not wanting to appear stagnant or unprogressive, you shift your attention to the petty tasks that don't overwhelm you. Doing these tasks gives you a sense of control over their outcomes. Consequently, you will be certain about what to expect.

However, in the long run, you put off your goals, and this limits your focus and productivity. This is because your actions aren't in synchronization with your goals and priorities anymore. If this fear continues over time, it causes you to lose sight of your main goals and pursue the wrong priorities instead. Don't mistake chasing just any priority as a sign of progress. Sometimes, it's the gateway to procrastination.

Fear of Judgment

There's no denying the fact that at some point in your life, you've weighed an action against another. You might not have realized that it is some kind of silent insecurity of yours—but in reality, that's what it is. There will always be times when your actions don't correspond with the expectations or demands of other people. This is because no two people are wired alike, and what you consider appropriate might not be for somebody else. However, rather than considering this eventuality, you eventually put off the task to avoid being judged badly by other people.

The fear of being judged makes you procrastinate because you're worried about what others think about you and your course of action. A typical example of this fear exists in everyday life. Say you go watch a friend stage a presentation for the first time. Now, as he mounts the stage, you notice the flare of his costume caught in the zipper, slightly baring his underpants. The right thing to do would be to try to get his attention to it or just go and set it right yourself. However, you plunge into a cognitive dilemma on the ethics of either action. You fear what people would say or think. You don't want anyone thinking you're insensitive, or rather fussy to the embarrassment it would cause your friend, so you hold back. You procrastinate doing the right thing until after his performance.

This instance portrays an example of what daily life holds. We sometimes overly immerse ourselves in the opinions of others that we fail to focus on our goals. We get more concerned about being on the good side of people than about pursuing our goals.

Action Triggers

Procrastination isn't always a result of intrinsic factors, as its causal factors can be extrinsic too. These extrinsic factors constitute what drives certain types of procrastination. The actions that trigger procrastination include but are not limited to:

The Infallibility Trigger

In the pursuit of goals, everyone strives to keep a clean track devoid of mistakes, or at least to minimize their tendency to make these mistakes. However, some people would settle for nothing less than perfect. This makes them get involved in performing an activity or task so cautiously that they forget how relevant it is to their primary goals.

Selected schools of thought are of the view that craving perfection infects the mind. It compared it to how people with anorexia nervosa view their reflections in mirrors. People with this condition starve themselves because they are afraid of putting on weight. They stare back at their reflections and see themselves as obese and overweight. Consequently, they starve themselves as a means of shedding the extra pounds. However, they aren't always obese or even fat. They're just so obsessed with not being overweight that their minds make them think they are.

In the same vein is infallibility. Perfectionists would rather indulge in petty activities with little risks of imperfections than long-term goals filled with uncertainties. In other cases, perfectionists are generally people unsatisfied with their progress. They never consider their actions to be good enough. Instead, they prefer continuously doing the exact same activity continuously until they reach their desired level of perfection. While in itself, perfectionism isn't necessarily a bad approach, it becomes one when it gets in the way of work. What perfectionists fail to discover is that perfection exists in different degrees—and like beauty, it is seen and appreciated differently. As such, the very things they deem imperfect could be the peak of perfection to another person.

The Over-Planning Trigger

It's one thing to set goals, and it's another thing to achieve them. Sometimes, we set goals and don't make room for changes that might occur in the long run. So, we end up making plans with fixed goals and priorities, but they are inflexible. While this isn't an entirely poor approach, it's very much limiting. Our goals are merely targets which may not always be under our control. Sometimes, some grow and need a bit of flexibility to be able to fit into these plans again. But when there is no room for flexibility, these specific prospering goals get mixed up with other goals that aren't as important, which leads to over-planning.

As proof of this, Pareto's Law or the 80-20 rule is of the opinion that in a population, a small amount of people is responsible for the higher prevalence of a specific trait in that population. Relating this to our activities, at least 80% of the results we get is on account of 20% of the tasks we indulge in. So, we must focus on getting the highest productivity rates with the least amount of tasks. We need to capitalize on the important 20% of our tasks and meet the 80% targets.

Over-planning is simply engulfing yourself in so many tasks that you end up thinking too much about everything. Consequently, this leads to minimal progress and inhibited productivity. However, don't make the mistake of using this as an excuse not to plan properly, as planning is an important factor in the pursuit of goals. If the pursuit of your goals revolves around planning and pre-planning to ensure your goals fit into your plans, you're giving yourself a reason to procrastinate.

It is advised to have a specific time to outline your goals and course of action — as this is your plan. Also, use only as much time as the planning process requires. Don't waste time on unnecessary planning. During the planning process, consider your goals and prioritize tasks with a higher turnover over petty, trivial tasks. The former constitutes 20%, which results in 80% of your productivity and, therefore, requires more work, so it should be done first. Doing this should thin down your plans and make room to allow any future changes. Finally, when you begin executing the plan, resist the urge to revisit your plans, and make changes. This is because the very act of revisiting your plans derails your focus. No one ever moved forward by looking back.

Also, it drains you of motivation, especially when you start having doubts about whether or not you made the right choices when you picked your goals. Eventually, you'll end up procrastinating because you feel the need to plan again.

The Overwork Trigger

Most of the time, stress and tiredness are the factors that give us the urge to procrastinate. When you feel stressed or tired, you are less able to make any effort. Also, you find it difficult to stay focused, and your productivity dwindles. This stress and tiredness can be a result of extrinsic and intrinsic factors, but more often than not, that factor is you. Sometimes, you're responsible for tiring yourself out by doing more work than necessary. Sure, there are times that call for this, but you rarely ever know when it's right to do this and when it isn't, or when to start and when to stop.

When you do too much work, you develop a higher tendency to procrastinate. Overworking tends to overwhelm you past the limits you are wired to attain, and once you exceed these limits, your body reacts unfavorably to more tasking work because it doesn't have the capacity to do it. This is why when you overwork, you find yourself attracted to little, irrelevant tasks.

When you overwork yourself, you consume your resources faster than normal. This results in a timeframe of retreat when you no longer feel enthused to work. This timeframe is characterized by inactivity and demoralization. You simply feel no urge whatsoever to keep on pursuing your goals and priorities. To avoid the horrors of overworking, you must understand your psychology and the limits to how far you can go. This puts you in pole position to schedule your goals for times when you are willing to work. Also, you will be able to find time in your everyday life to unwind. If this is done right, you avoid stress and avert the problems that come with overworking.

Behavioral Triggers

Has it ever occurred to you that your tendency to procrastinate might be because of your behavior? Well, now, you do. Our behavior is simply the way we react to things.

In regard to focus and productivity, our behavior towards work determines whether or not we're likely to procrastinate in the long run. The reason for procrastination could be the result of certain behavioral patterns. These behaviors might bear no significance to you, and may not necessarily seem like triggers for procrastination. This is because your habits are so deeply embedded in you that you don't always see it. It is your way of expression, your psyche. As such, it is harder to identify.

In any scenario, the way you react, whether it is instinctively based or emotionally motivated, isn't always a result of careful thinking. Sometimes, your behavior is birthed beyond the conscious mind, deep in your subconscious.

Therefore, behavioral triggers are any habitual patterns that result in states of incapability. These behavioral patterns include, but are not limited to, the following:

Low Self-Esteem

While it isn't practically sound to praise yourself too hard, you shouldn't put yourself down either. Self-esteem accounts for the way you judge yourself and your abilities. Self-esteem puts you in a state where your progress is determined by how you perceive yourself. Hence, the lesser you think of yourself, the slimmer your chances to progress, and vice versa. No one ever grew with this mindset.

Having poor self-esteem gives you a weakened mindset, which affects the way you look at work. This way, every task appears more daunting than it really is, and you constantly feel incapable of handling it. When this feeling sets in, you become more likely to procrastinate. And since procrastination is the enemy of success, the after-effects of putting away your priorities could come back to haunt you, causing you to shrink deeper into yourself and procrastinate even more. Eventually, you lose focus on your goals. Also, productivity doesn't come without a pursuit, so there's none of it, too.

Low self-esteem could also make you resort to self-targeted criticism, where you constantly blame your incapability as the reason for unproductivity.

Over-Expectancy

The reason many people give in to procrastination is that they expect too much of themselves. Expectations are simply the eventualities of the future by which you should shape your present. They serve as the measuring instruments used to determine how far we should go. However, you could sometimes get too involved with seeing the future that you plan a little too much. This accounts for why sometimes, you expect so much that you set goals that are beyond your reach and resources. You thus deprive yourself of the opportunity to attain those goals because you haven't got the resources you set for it.

For instance, imagine a one-year-old child trying to reach for a glass on a table that is 20 meters taller than he is. As far as he stretches, he will still be unable to reach it. And, if he eventually manages to get a hold of the glassware, he may be unable to take it off successfully, or worse, may end up breaking it.

This example highlights over-expectancy. Somehow, you try to reach for something clearly beyond you—and most of the time, you are responsible for putting it beyond your reach. You end up unsuccessful in reaching your goals. This causes you to lose motivation, and you feel like giving up. And when you don't exactly feel like giving up, you resort to putting off your goals to first gather the resources that would help you better reach them. This, unknown to you, leads to procrastination.

Emotional Triggers

We can all agree that sometimes, our tendency to procrastinate is based on our feelings. The emotional part of ourselves plays as much a role in our decisions as our cognition, which explains why certain judgments we make are based on them.

Our daily lives are characterized by challenges and changes that confront us. Each and every one of these challenges, incidents, changes, etc. have tendencies to affect us in ways that elicit an emotional reaction from us. The way we react emotionally determines our tendency to procrastinate. We've all felt some painful emotions in the past, some so painful sometimes that we block them out of our minds. These painful experiences are often a result of poor choices we made, or due to a lack of resourcefulness in tackling challenges effectively. Consequently, we plunge into a state of emotional upheaval because we feel powerless in front of the challenges that face us. Due to the emotional turmoil in which we find ourselves, it becomes easier to procrastinate than get important stuff done.

Many emotional states can be credited to be triggers of procrastination as a result of their influence on human life and overall productivity. These emotions include:

The Feeling of Being Helpless

This is a common feeling for us any time we try to do more than what we usually do. Every person has a distinct threshold of work they can do at a particular time. This describes the normal limits within which they can work. However, when this threshold is exceeded, we tend to feel overwhelmed. Once this feeling of being engulfed in too much work sets in, we find ourselves distanced from our goals and priorities. This is because our focus would waver from the strain of doing too much in an abnormal timeframe, thus causing our efficiency to reduce.

As a result of overstimulation and the stress of working too hard, we become less attentive to our priorities and goals, making us work on petty, irrelevant tasks instead. In other words, we end up procrastinating. When we feel overwhelmed, it becomes an extremely arduous task to keep chasing our goals. Hence, we slack, and this causes us to procrastinate.

The only way out of this deadly cycle of procrastination is to understand the limits we can go to and tackle the most important 20% of our tasks within that time frame.

The Feeling of Inadequacy

When we fail in regard to breaking off the cycle of procrastination, we end up struggling with the feeling of being inadequate. Once this insecurity gets the best of us, we begin to consider ourselves practically unable and unimaginative in tackling the problems and challenges that inhibit the pursuit of our goals. As we flail helplessly in a puddle of inadequacy, we might feel tempted to redirect our focus and re-strategize completely. However, as much as this might seem to do us good and grant us a sense of satisfaction, all it does is make us busy. We end up indulging in tasks that add no real value to our priorities and goals.

The Feeling of Frustration

Every person can testify to having felt frustrated before. This feeling usually arises as a result of our inability to make significant progress in pursuit of our goals or our failure to meet a target. It's easy to get frustrated when we feel unable to accomplish a task or meet our expectations. Simply put, frustration is the outcome of an unexpected twist. After we make our plays and give it our best shot, we hope it goes in the direction we planned. However, it doesn't always happen like this due to many different reasons.

In essence, the feeling of frustration has its good sides, as long as it doesn't get out of hand because if it does, it then becomes harder to keep a firm grip on our emotions. Eventually, it could cause us to resort to an emotional state where we cringe at work due to the fear of failure. This could ultimately ruin our chances and efforts at pursuing our goals.

The Feeling of Boredom

This is arguably the most common procrastination trigger in this category. When you feel bored, you're highly likely to want to procrastinate as a means of avoiding the very things that bore you. This can happen when you take on tasks with a comfortable and continuous pattern that goes on for a long time. It often springs from the tiredness of continuing in a pattern no longer considered as appealing as it once was.

To break the jinx of frustration, you need to add more stimulating tasks to your schedule. Engage in tasks that you find interesting and that are valuable to your goal. Work is best done when it is seen as play. This reduces your dread for it and gives you a sense of objectivity in your approach.

The Deficiency Factor

Sometimes, your tendency to procrastinate is determined by what you lack. For instance, lacking the know-how to chase your goals might cause you to put them off until you're resourceful enough to chase them. This implies that procrastination is sometimes triggered as a behavioral mechanism in response to the absence of certain necessary factors. These necessary factors could be intrinsic or extrinsic, while some are cognitive and emotionally-based, and others are physical traits. These factors include:

Deficiency of Focus

It's not surprising that focus emerges as a necessary factor needed to combat procrastination, and the lack of focus in any goal-driven pursuit is just as futile as any expected productivity is fictitious. We tend to procrastinate because we have no focus.

But no one is naturally without focus, so how did we lose it in the first place? Focus is lost in a number of ways, including multitasking, overworking, lack of clarity, etc. All these give room for distractions that cloud our focus and reorient our priorities to less relevant indulgences. In reality, the focus isn't literally lost. In fact, focus, like any other abstract phenomenon, simply revolves around certain rules of engagement. Whatever captures your attention gets your focus. As such, your focus shifts as your attention shifts. Thus, to effectively combat procrastination, you need to pay attention to the right things and put your focus in the right direction.

Deficiency of Purpose

As much as the focus is important to overcoming procrastination, the latter needs an anchor to hold still. A purpose is what keeps your focus steady and avoids you from procrastinating. Without a clearly defined purpose, it's impossible to follow a specific course of action, as it gives you a sense of direction and a sense of knowing what you want and why you are doing it. It's the propellant that keeps you running. This is the only way to retain focus in the long run.

Deficiency of Direction

A famous saying states that "a person who knows his destination never misses the way." This implies that a sense of direction is critical to remaining focused and curbing procrastination. If you have no sense of direction, it becomes nearly impossible to pursue your goals seamlessly. Every other path that you stumble upon seems to be the right path, but it isn't necessarily so.

Having no direction whatsoever makes you susceptible to focusing on indulgences that aren't worthwhile to your aims and that produce little to no result. Thus, you end up spending quality time and energy on things that won't be profitable in the long run.

Lack of Resources

Not having the resources to pursue your goals can prove to be a big hindrance. Not only does it affect you intrinsically by working you up emotionally and cognitively, but it also affects you extrinsically, and you become powerless. When you lack the necessary resources to give you momentum, you become helpless in the pursuit of your goals. This would cause you to play to the gallery and indulge in less productive tasks as a means of biding your time to re-strategize.

The best way to overcome procrastination caused by a lack of resources is to equip yourself and clear out your deficiencies. Find a way to gain the required skill sets, acquire the necessary physical resources, etc., rather than settle for something less.

Chapter 2: Tackling Procrastination

Like all other behavior, procrastination can be managed and overcome. Below are some useful tips on how to help you manage and overcome your urge to procrastinate.

Understand Procrastination and Your Connection to It

If you are in denial about the fact that you procrastinate, you won't be able to get over this problem. The only way to get over a problem is by recognizing you have one in the first place. Only once you've done this will you be able to find ways to overcome it.

First, understand the concept of procrastination; that it isn't the act of unwillingness to do something, but rather the act of neglecting important tasks for less important ones. This might be reflected in your tendency to prioritize a smaller, more enjoyable task over an arduous, more important one. However, when you simply put off an important task because you feel like you would be better able to tackle it at another time, it isn't necessarily procrastination, especially when it is done for a good reason, such as freeing up your schedule, not wanting to overwork or over-plan, etc. You should be careful to avoid making this a habit by making up excuses and setting yourself up for a cycle of procrastination.

Next, be deliberate about your goals and know how to prioritize. If you make goals of lower value tasks, you're still procrastinating. Also, try to clear your schedule and meet your daily goals. Try not to leave important tasks hanging for long. It could lead to procrastination and for no reason at all.

Manage Your Indulgences to Prevent Distractions

Take note of possible distractions and how they affect you. Sometimes, our indulgences don't look like distractions even though they are, and this somehow triggers procrastination. Such indulgences could include:

- Checking emails and social media when you should be focused on other important tasks - Now, there's no ban on checking your social media or emails, just don't let them be the distraction that keeps important tasks at bay. And owing to their rather addictive nature, they're likely to distract you if prioritized over your goals, making you procrastinate. You should know when it is right to use them and when it's time to work. Set limits.

- Taking tea or coffee breaks - It's no secret that many of us need a caffeine boost to get down to business. However, don't allow the making this to be the reason you put an important task on hold.

- Accepting intrusive work and people - Just because you feel the need to humor people, it doesn't mean you should allow it to get the better of you. Your goals are more important to you than every other person's. Don't go out of your way to take on other people's tasks or indulge people instead of pursuing your goals. You can find other time for that.

- Biding your time/waiting for the perfect mood - Sometimes, we make silly assertions of needing to be in the 'right mood' or 'time' to be able to do certain tasks. While this might be true to a certain degree, most often than not, it's a sign of procrastination. The best time to begin working on your assignments is when you still have plenty of time to get it done.

Identify the Reason You Procrastinate and Fix It

After admitting to yourself that you procrastinate, the second step is to identify why you procrastinate. Like every other problem, you have to identify why it occurs in order to be able to fix it. As a matter of fact, the root of every problem is the key to knowing why it occurs. Hence, in order to fix procrastination, you need to identify and understand why it happens. It could be as a result of its many different triggers. Also, finding a task not enjoyable and arduous could make you put it off. Instead of falling into the trap or urge to procrastinate, try approaching the task with resoluteness. Reevaluate and reposition your views. View the task instead as the only inhibition keeping you from doing what you enjoy. Get it done and over with, without letting anything get in your way.

Also, allowing yourself to get carried away by distractions can also make you procrastinate. The more time and energy you spend on social media and peer interaction, the more your uncompleted tasks linger. And there's nothing as demoralizing as switching from an entertainment spree to work. This is most likely why you procrastinate. Tackle your tasks first and reward your labor with as much time on social media or peer interaction as your schedule allows. Just don't let the latter become a priority to you over the former. The entertainment you gain from these indulgences is only momentary; undone tasks are not.

Poor planning and disorganization can also trigger procrastination. If you have no sense of organization and are prone to poor planning, you might as well have found your procrastination trigger. When you have a sound sense of organization, you know better than to prioritize less important tasks. This helps you better plan your activities in a concurrent, flexible order that makes work seamless. By simply improving your organization and planning skills, you are able to overcome procrastination as it is key in helping you target the important 20% of your activities.

Take Timed Breaks as You Work

We have already discussed that being overwhelmed is one of the main triggers of procrastination. As we are human, we are bound to feel tiredness as we do our work. And the more tired we become, the more our focus and productivity dwindle. When we become overwhelmed, we naturally seek a way out, hence our tendency to procrastinate. It is vital that you have an understanding of how your body works and know it needs to be refreshed regularly to stay productive. Plan your schedule to include breaks in-between tasks. This should help you rest and refresh your body and mind to get ready for another task. It also helps decrease your urge to procrastinate.

Avoid Perfectionism

At times, the best way to conquer procrastination is to know that perfection doesn't always fit the picture we have in mind. If you keep chasing perfection, you're more likely to be overwhelmed by a task, and when you keep doing the same thing over and over again expecting a different result like an improvement in perfection, you're only setting yourself up for a cycle of procrastination. You end up dwelling on one task for so long that it gets in the way of others. It could also cause you to doubt yourself. Slowly, fears of failure set in, causing you to crave some level of comfort and enjoyment. You end up doing tasks you feel capable of doing in order to regain a sense of satisfaction even though it contributes nothing to your goals.

Avoid Multitasking

As much as multitasking can be helpful in covering more work in less time, it may lead to distractions or overworking, and these two are only good at making you procrastinate. Instead of multitasking, focus on finishing your tasks one at a time. In other words, stick to a single task at a time. It saves you from distractions and errors that could happen as you divide your attention between different tasks. If you ever feel the urge to multitask, consider its end results — errors that you will make you spend more time and effort to fix.

Stay Mindful of Your Tasks

Staying mindful of your tasks involves taking responsibility for your activities. When you're mindful of your activities, you see them for what they really are; stepping stones in the pursuit of your goals. When you are in this mindset, you don't succumb to any excuses whatsoever and do about anything to keep yourself from errors. This doesn't mean you become obsessed with perfection. No - this just means you are being cautious in pursuing your goals.

With you having now gone through this, it is evident that the causes of procrastination can be summarized into the following groups:

1. Failure to get organized

2. Failure to have the right attitude and mindset

3. Not knowing how to deal with stress

4. Suffering from anxiety

5. Unclear thinking

What this basically means is that for you to solve your procrastination issues, you need to deal with the five points above.

Chapter 3: Getting Organized

When one is considered organized, it simply means they are systematic and orderly in the way they approach and do things. Organization involves planning, managing your time properly, and sticking to your plan.

Most of us will jot down a list of items to buy before we walk into a supermarket, or even if not, we are likely to do a mental inventory of our supplies before making purchases. You select a day within the week to do your laundry as well as your housekeeping to ensure that your place is tidy. At the office, we gather in boardrooms at specific times to discuss and come up with strategies to move our business forward.

Before you take a trip to Paris or a safari in Kenya, you inquire about the costs, make bookings, and set a travel date. Before you send your daughter or son to school, you make inquiries about a series of things before settling for a particular institution; of course, the place will be one that you feel provides the best academic education for your child, but also a place where your child will benefit from overall growth and development. When you are due for a job interview, you try and get to the place before the designated time, and by then, you should have already done a bit of research about the organization and of course, familiarized yourself with the position.

These instances are all elements of organizing; to plan in advance for an activity or event so that when you begin your tasks, it is easy, clear, and successful.

So, why should you be organized? Experience and research have shown that people who are organized are generally more successful at what they do, accomplish more than those who are not, tend to have more 'free' time, and lead overall happier lives. When you make a plan and stick to it, you are able to manage your life effectively and lead a fulfilling and happy life. By being organized, your time is well-managed, and your activities are planned and predictable, which makes them easier, so you will always do things to completion, and your reward will be a happier, more satisfying life.

Therefore, if you are one who is not organized and always finds himself in a mess when handling things, you need to start planning and bring order to your life. Most times, constraints and lateness or even failing to know something you should be linked directly to deficiency or lack of organization.

Next, let's look at the question of time and its management and why it is key to being organized.

Time Management

Time management involves the prudent use of time by knowing how you are spending it, organizing your time and activities, and committing to what you have planned your time for. It helps to do things IN time if you want to avoid the headache of last-minute pursuits.

It is applicable in all aspects of our lives - professional, personal, and social, so it should be a habit that is embraced and treated dearly. When we manage our time well, we tend to succeed in whatever we are doing, and we lead a happier life with minimal stress.

Managing your time involves looking at the commitments in your life and deciding which is more important than the other, and then arranging, prioritizing, or replacing these commitments so that the most important is at the top of your to-do list.

Also, time management is about simplifying your life by making it easy to get things done. The more non-important commitments you put aside, the more time you will have to devote to more important things. Designating a time for everything you want to do makes things a lot easier.

Most of us are familiar with the cliché wise terms about time, "Time is money," "Time lost shall never be recovered," etc. Time is the single most important commodity in our lives; if you use it wisely, you will cherish and enjoy your time on earth, but if you waste it, you will end up with regrets. Plan your time to the millisecond and use your time prudently.

Develop a habit of planning, using, and sticking to your program to understand the benefits of time management. It is the first and major step towards realizing your dream of leading an organized life and being successful in whatever you pursue. Once you have perfected the art of time management and made it part of your life, the next thing is to know when to say NO!

Time is such a tricky thing. Sometimes, we have so much of it (though often these seem to be negative times), and other times, we just can't get enough. Managing it—well, that's always been fiddly. Thankfully we've got a few Mindset Hacks that may do just the trick.

We've gathered together some time-saving tips that will help you manage your time like a pro. Many of them are, like the best advice, simple things we've seen others do and are just efficient ways to use a few handy tools that you may already in your environment to maximize your time-usage. Here is a handy list of tips and tricks that we've compiled for you:

1. **Time journal** - Think of this as the 'audit phase' portion of improving your time-management skills. Keep track of how you are spending your hours via apps or a good old-fashioned paper planner. While the paper doesn't have all the bells and whistles that you might like, it comes already organized for documenting skills. This means you don't have to spend time learning a new app if you just want to get started with logging where your time goes.

2. **Choose commitments wisely** - This is actually quite important. If you are always selecting very time-sensitive tasks that you find overly debilitating, this can affect your overall productivity. Try to opt for work-tasks that don't drain you as much whenever possible. Don't skip over the difficult ones completely, of course, as generally, these complicated tasks are how we learn to do more. That said, everyone has their own special skills, and there is nothing wrong with keeping them sharp by taking commitments that won't drain you daily.

3. **Keep emails brief** - A personal favorite. This one can save you an immense amount of time. Keep your email responses lean and mean. Just the facts that the recipient needs, no more, and no less. Often you can find yourself writing tiny novels at work when it's easily avoided with a bit of practice. The next time you find yourself writing an email with a length approaching the last Stephen King novel, then stop. Sit on it for a day and then open it again. Ask yourself, 'How can I say the same thing in 5 or 6 sentences?'. This trick also works when sending an emotional email at work (a huge no-no) by letting you step away to view the contents of the email the next morning. This lets you take out anything unnecessary, including useless information, speculation about the day, or emotions if you find it hard to work with another person

in your company. When it comes to emails, save yourself a world of time by sticking to just the facts!

4. **Typing practice** - Are you a hunt-and-peck typist? Downloading some typing-tutor software or utilizing any number of free typing resources online can be of immense help to you if you are working with a computer every day. The average typing speed for non-IT professionals is typically around 40 words per minute. By increasing your speed to IT-level typing (around 70-90 words per minute), you can reduce your time at the computer by half and put that time in other places as needed! Be sure to start training your new typing skills today!

5. **Use alarms** - Your smartphone has some very simple alarm functions that you can utilize to schedule your tasks. That said, if you are using a computer at work and have Outlook, take the time to synchronize it with your smartphone. It makes scheduling tasks a BREEZE and will give you an alert 15 minutes before said task so that you can be ready (time is adjustable, and you can dismiss these alerts or 'snooze' them if you need to.

6. **Templates -** These are excellent when writing novels, reports, and any number of other complex items that we need to wizard-up in the workplace. A template can save you time by allowing you to direct the necessary data at a much faster rate than you could collate on your own. As a

bonus, the more that you use them, the less you may find that you rely on them, having filed away the mental order in your subconscious. If you don't have templates for reports and such already available at your workplace, a quick Google search can net you a number of templates for just about anything. Take advantage of this and save yourself hours of outlining. It's worth it.

7. **Dictation** - Are you not a huge fan of typing—be it due to arthritis, carpal tunnel, or even an old grudge with a typing teacher—you are not quite ready to let go of? Not a problem. Programs like Dragon: NaturallySpeaking can learn the particular cadences of your voice to make not only typing but system commands into a much more pleasant experience. This particular software has been around for years and as such, adapts to your voice with very little training at all. Best of all, the professional version comes with macros, a feature which lets you 'record' doing something a little more complex, say opening a particular folder and set of documents followed by starting up the music player for a particular playlist, which you can assign specific voice commands to. Macros actually record where you click your mouse and what actions you take, so it can be a very, very useful tool in your time-saving panoply. Remember to keep the music to instrumentals, of course, as the computer *will* be listening for your commands, but with a little setup

program of this nature can greatly improve your productivity.

8. **Start EARLY at the same time each day** - While you might not like this one at first, getting up and ensuring that you come to work earlier is a great habit to get yourself into. Tell yourself, "On-time is *late*," and start ensuring that you are always at work 20 minutes early so that you have time to relax for a cup of coffee, maybe read the daily news (important for the socialization factors at work), and to review your workload before leaping into the fray! Developing this habit now can really help improve overall productivity, as you won't feel rushed every morning but rather feel relaxed, refreshed, and ready-to-go!

9. **Don't get bogged down with details** - If you find yourself getting stuck on small tasks, move on to the next task, and make a note to return to the previous. Sometimes tiny details can get us stuck when there are still things that we can be doing in the immediate time. If you have structured out your work, then there are a number of components that you can focus on. Think of it like clockwork. There are many tiny cogs and springs making up the whole, and each one has its own importance. Focus on what you CAN do. If you are still rather worried about missing some of the more important tasks then worry no more, we have a chapter coming up

about prioritization hacks that will help you know what you can put off and what you should work on right away.

10. **Utilize downtime** - Are you having trouble loading internet pages? Are you waiting for an email from someone who is also working on the same project? Utilize your downtime. There is always something that you can be doing. Choose another item from your task list that you can begin on. Outline the next steps for when you complete the stalled task. At the very least, you can review your current progress until you get the go-ahead to move forward. Be creative; you know that there is work that you can do and that it can make a huge difference when you are working on a deadline. Make use of that downtime now, and you'll have more free time later.

11. **Come in early** - Every now and again, a great way to get ahead at work is a simple method. Come in early. You'll have fewer distractions in the office, more time to work, and a refreshed morning-mindset that will allow you to tackle the toughest of problems. Besides, no matter how blind we think they sometimes might be, your boss notices things like this. A minimal time investment now could mean a promotion or at the very least, fewer instances of having to work on the weekend—just something to consider.

12. **Don't immediately reply to emails** - Email is a wonderful medium for quick communication; however, it can also be a maddening distraction. Try deciding times in advance when you will answer emails. Generally, we get a popup when an email comes in with the name and subject present. Take advantage of this by advising your boss and co-workers to put 'Urgent' in the subject line if the matter is something that must be dealt with immediately. This way, you know what can and cannot wait, and you can devote all of your focus to your work.

13. **Batch related tasks** - If you have a number of tasks to do and many of them are similar or in the same category, then do them in category related batches. For instance, if you need to run 2 reports, contact 3 clients, and email 2 clients, it is a waste of time to run 1 report, email a client, etc. Do all the reports at once, do all the calls at once, same with the emails. The reasoning behind this is that there is a different mentality associated with various types of tasks. It is more efficient to do them in related batches so that you don't have to switch mindsets constantly. Try doing your work in related batches and see just how much time you can truly save. You'll be happier for it.

14. **Energize - (caffeine or fruit sugars)** - If you don't abuse it, caffeine and fruit sugars can be your friend. When you need to work quickly and with extra alertness, then be sure not to skip the coffee. Fruit sugars work as

well, so if you are not a fan of coffee or tea, start your morning with some apple slices and honey. This can give you that extra 'go!' to help you tackle the most that you can during your workday (with the added bonus of tasty beverages or fruits!).

15. **Determine your optimal schedule** - Everyone has time during the day or evening when they are working at their best. Do you know what times are for you? It might be worthwhile to take note of the times when it seems that you are getting the most done. Knowledge of this timeframe can help you, as you can assign yourself your most difficult tasks during these hours so that you can grind at them when you are at your most efficient. Give yourself a productivity/time audit and make the most of this technique!

16. **Telecommute when possible** - Working from home saves money for your place of employment and also makes you more productive. There is a level of relaxation that comes from a home that is good for boosting confidence and performance, and you simply cannot reproduce it in the office. Plus, a time that you save commuting is a time that you can spend on yourself!

17. **Ditch that difficult task until after lunch** - If you have been struggling all morning with a particular task, consider moving to another task and returning to the

problematical one after lunch. Once you've eaten, you will feel more relaxed and energized, and the time that you spent separating your mind from the problematical task will ensure that you will return to it with a fresh perspective and attitude. If you can put it off until after lunch, then consider this approach. You'd be amazed at what your mind can come up within a problem-solving scenario once you've given it a little slack.

18. **Big, obnoxious desk clock** - Get yourself a large, perhaps even silly-large desk clock. Yes, we realize that you can check the time on your work computer or your phone, but this is a mental hack that we are suggesting here. Having a large clock in your view will make you acutely aware of the time at all times! This will help make sure that you realize how much time you are spending on particular items and make you mindful of upcoming items that require your attention later in the day. Give it a try, and you'll see. A little time awareness goes a long way!

Know When to Say "NO"

How often do you say "NO" to an unscheduled meeting or last-minute date? When was the last time you said "NO" to the craving of buying another handbag or running to the nearest Wal-Mart to buy items that you already have or do not need just because there is a big sale?

Being able to say know is an important component of getting your life organized. Often, we find ourselves bending over backward for family members and colleagues at work, especially our bosses and friends, and we end up doing things we had not planned to do because they asked us to. If you are a victim of this and want to get your life in order, start saying "NO" to activities that you have not planned for. Of course, this doesn't include emergencies and critical, unforeseeable issues.

The moment you start tolerating unplanned or unscheduled activities, it eats into the time meant for other things and leaves some tasks uncompleted because you decided to compromise. You end up piling up work or tasks that you would have otherwise finished just because you could not utter the word "NO!"

Declining unscheduled tasks will free up so much of your time and will relieve you of mental clutter and unnecessary workload.

Try saying "NO" from today and see how much easier your life is; you will have enough time to do the core activities you need to be doing, whether professionally, socially, or in your personal life.

When you already have a microwave that works well, say "NO" to the impulse urging you to purchase another one just because it has a price reduction. If your mother or sister did not tell you that they needed your help with something in advance, do not do so when they call you in the last second- dedicate that time instead of doing the things that you have planned on doing.

When you learn to say "NO," always do things one at a time, just like we are going to see next. If you want to be organized, multitasking is not necessarily the way to go.

Do One Thing at a Time

Doing one thing at a time means concentrating on a task and completing it before embarking on another. Most of the time, we find ourselves overwhelmed by work or chores because we take on more than we can handle at once.

Handling activities one after the other means giving all your undivided attention to the one you are handling; you will find yourself doing it much faster and better than if you were handling five tasks at the same time. Handling one activity at a time will make you more productive, and ultimately, you will be more resourceful.

Overloading yourself with tasks will often result in not completing some of the things taken on. However, if completed, you may find errors or in hindsight, discover that you missed something that you otherwise wouldn't have had you been concentrating on one task at a time.

You do not want to be preparing food in the kitchen and watching American Idol at the same time - you will end up missing a great performance while running to the kitchen, fearful that your onions will burn because you got enthralled by a singer on the show.

Similarly, you do not want to schedule an appointment shortly after you plan on doing a presentation, as you will almost always not give one the attention it deserves. If you take this approach, you will end unprepared, disorderly, and unprofessional.

If you decide to do one thing at a time, you will find yourself better organized, and pressures of running late or not meeting deadlines will be greatly mitigated. If adopted and applied effectively, this habit will lead to more completed, successful tasks.

Once you have resorted to finishing a task before taking on another, you will know the value of not procrastinating; do that thing now, not tomorrow, not in ten minutes - RIGHT NOW!

Do Not Postpone; Do It Now

Many people tend to defer tasks to "another time," ultimately ending up with piles of uncompleted work.

Procrastination is the enemy of achieving anything, so organization is key. Highly organized people do not postpone things that should be done; they do them now, before moving on to the next task.

You need to actively develop a habit of doing things when they are due; postponing will get you in a rut of piling up work and not completing the things you need to be doing. This habit can be very debilitating and can critically affect one's productivity if not nipped in the bud.

If you want to get your life organized, start doing things now—not tomorrow or in so and so minutes. By tackling and completing things when they are due, you avoid piling up work and thus become more productive.

The more you do things on time without postponing them, the more organized you get, and the better your life is going to be.

Next, let's see why the much talked about a to-do list is important for highly organized people.

Keep a To-Do List

List down everything you intend to do on a piece of paper or electronic device like your smartphone. If adopted in your day to day activities, a to-do list will help you get truly organized.

Any highly organized and successful person will tell you that a to-do list is a compulsory component of managing their lives and is important in keeping them organized.

When you have listed down the things you need to do, you are highly unlikely to forget to do something as the list is intended to be used as a reference and to know what action to prioritize first. Also, it is recommended to have only one to-do list, as keeping more than one can lead to disorganization if misplaced or lost.

A to-do list can be made on a computer, your wall calendar, your phone, and the like—and with advancements in technology, the electronic devices even come with reminder capabilities.

Anyone who wants to get organized must keep a to-do list for reference; it is your planning log. Once you have a list of activities that need to be done, managing your day becomes so much easier.

In the next section, we will look at how de-cluttering is a habit to adopt if you want to get organized.

Set Aside a De-Cluttering Day

Clutter is all the mess around your office, on your desk, in your house, or in your closet caused as a result of not putting your things in order.

De-clutter regularly; set aside a day and time every week to re-arrange and get your office or house in order. Get rid of items that you do not need like clothes that you no longer wear, and clear your desk of papers that are no longer useful to you.

At all costs, avoid placing things where they do not belong; once an item is in the wrong place, this may end up leading to a mess.

Repeated actions become habits, and habits are really hard to kick—so do not get in the habit of throwing things around and causing a mess.

Organized people regularly get rid of things that they no longer need to create more room for them and avoid the mess that comes with piling up unnecessary items.

Mind clutter is also an area that you will need to work on; you could easily be suffering from mental chaos! Take time to evaluate your mental state to avoid cluttering your mind. Spend some time to relax and to clear your mind of unnecessary thoughts and worries that may be clouding your judgment. Do this in conjunction with the other tips.

Clear your life of things that you no longer need; you will lead a much better and organized life devoid of clutter.

Advance planning is integral to getting organized; let's find out why next.

Plan in Advance

Planning in advance will give you a head start for the next day - always plan in advance if you want to elevate your life to the level of highly organized people. At the end of every day, jot down your activities for the next day.

Schedule things to be done the following day, so that by the time you rest your head at night, you already have an outline of the things to do the next day, and at what time.

All highly organized and successful people claim to plan things in advance, some even weeks before. Planning ahead gives your life predictability and allows you to manage your time more effectively.

To be more organized, embrace advance planning and make it a habit to be ready ahead of time; you will rid your life of surprises and unnecessary pressures that may arise due to lack of foresight.

Taking the simple step of planning ahead will significantly minimize the likelihood of being ambushed by duties or activities. Do this, and you will notice a big change for the better in the management of your life, and things will be a lot easier to accomplish since you are mentally prepared for them.

Planning ahead entails scheduling your activities for the future and putting time restraints on when to do them. If you are seeking self-organization, find out why schedules and deadlines are important.

Have Schedules and Deadlines

A schedule is a roster of things to do and at what time, while deadlines are the time when the activities you have scheduled are due for completion.

Anyone who wants to get organized must schedule their activities and make a deadline for all of them; otherwise, you will never attain an organized state of mind. Schedules and deadlines are basically tethers that keep us in place and prevent us from wandering off aimlessly.

Lack of scheduling means no clear cut things to do, and this will ultimately result in confusion and poor performance. Deadlines are important for time management while you are tackling your activities or duties, whatever they may be. Without deadlines, most things would not be done at all, or would they be completed on time.

Highly organized people keep schedules and set deadlines which they abide by religiously; please adopt these important habits if you want to change your life profoundly.

While scheduling leaves room for any last-minute thing that may arise, more often than not, important things that you have not planned for will arise. With schedules, you do not promise or over-estimate what you will deliver.

Next, let's look at how to prioritize the items in your schedule for a better and more optimal organization.

Prioritize

To prioritize things in your life means to categorize them from the most important to the least important and to pursue them in that order, with the most important being attended to first.

Knowing what is more important than the other is critical in the pursuit of self-organization; once you know the order of things in your life, everything falls in place quite easily.

If you are trying to get more organized, start prioritizing your daily activities for optimal performance and productivity. Start filtering through your to-do list and log them in their order of priority.

Tackling activities in their order of importance will reduce the pressure that arises with backlogs, or nearing deadlines without having finished a task. Your order of priority could be based on the due date of the work, the size of the work, how critical is it, etc.

Once you prioritize things, put in some "me time," as we will discuss next.

Me Time

Organized people always set aside time for themselves to self-reflect and rest, enabling them to rejuvenate and re-energize themselves.

If you are working towards realizing your dream of organized life, 'me time' is very important.

Regularly set aside some time to spend by yourself without the hassles of work or the attention of your home; just be by yourself. Try to dedicate a slot once a week to have your time; half a day or a full day is ideal for achieving maximum results.

Your time will help you clear your mind and have a clarity of purpose; during this time, take up a relaxing activity like yoga or meditation, which have been proven to be great ways to get you relaxed. Alternatively, go for a bike ride through a quiet cycling track, take a walk in the woods, or go to the spa for a relaxing massage and pampering session.

If you can't get away, you may opt to read a book or do a few rounds in the swimming pool—after some 'me time,' you will be amazed at how much better you feel and how productive you will get.

'Me time' will give you the energy for a more structured and productive life; in other words, an organized life!

Sleep

Lack of sleep is a major problem in our society. Insomnia is thought to be the number one problem in the USA. More than 30% of Americans find it hard to fall asleep every night, and half of the adult population claim to have sleeping problems a few days of the week. Furthermore, almost half of those interviewed said that sleeping during the day affected their daily activities, and these problems are getting worse each passing day. Between 2000 and 2004, the number of adults using sleeping pills doubled. Also, the percentage of kids aged between 1 and 19 who use sleeping pills rose to 85%.

In 2008, prescription drugs to induce sleep reached 56 million. This is not something surprising in a society that worships productivity as well as activity. Society today is against rest and relaxation; we are constantly in a rat race. To us, resting means watching TV, browsing the net, or being occupied by an electronic device. Without enough sleep, you cannot be healthy. Why is sleep important for our bodies?

Sleep is responsible for the basic maintenance and repair of the neurological, endocrine, and immune and digestive systems. In the evening, melatonin increases naturally and aids in protecting against infections. This is why one is likely to catch the flu or a cold if they fail to have enough sleep for a couple of nights. Sleep is so important that absolute deprivation of sleep has proven to be fatal. A lab experiment showed that rats that are denied the chance to rest die within two or three weeks.

Having enough sleep has several benefits, including:

- Memory improvement

- Enhanced athleticism

- Boosting the overall mood and body energy

- Boosting immunity

- Increasing tolerance to stress

Having less than six hours of sleep every night is linked to low grade chronic inflammation and deterioration of insulin resistance. It also increases the risk of obesity, diabetes, as well as cardiovascular diseases. When we don't get enough sleep, our ability to think, handle stress, and maintain a healthy immune system is greatly affected. Also, it affects our emotions. Being deprived of sleep causes the following:

- Weak immune system - research conducted at the University of California revealed that less sleep weakens the immune system's response to diseases and injuries.

- Weight gain and obesity - studies have shown that even being deprived of sleep for a single night can lead to major changes in appetite and the intake of food. Other studies have also shown that it affects tolerance to carbs and sensitivity to insulin. Also, lack of sleep causes fatty liver disease.

- A decline in cognition - lack of sleep affects the short-term and long-term working memory as well as the degeneration of nerve cells. All these negatively impact our ability to think and function clearly.

- Mood and mental health - sleeplessness is linked to depression. Insufficient sleep shuts down the pre-frontal cortex and can cause several psychological conditions.

- Reduced lifespan

Using sleeping pills can cause dependence, insomnia, drowsiness, memory loss, and much more. Medication to induce sleep should only be used as a last resort. To make yourself fall asleep easier, you need to reduce your exposure to artificial light, as unnatural light disrupts your circadian rhythm and prevents sleep. A study revealed that the light emitted from alarm clocks and other digital devices suppresses the production of melatonin. To avoid exposure to light:

- Avoid being in front of a computer at least two hours before you go to bed.

- Use blackout shades to make your bedroom darker.

- Switch off all digital devices that glow or emit any kind of light.

- Use a sleeping mask if necessary.

Also, do not eat too much or go to bed too hungry. When you sleep, you go through a one and half hour cycle of non-REM sleep, followed by REM sleep. However, within the half-hour cycles, the ratio of non-REM sleep fluctuates across the night. Between 11 pm and 3 am, most of the cycles are composed of deep non-REM sleep and very little REM sleep.

In the second half (between 3 am and 7 am), the balance does change, and the cycles are comprised of more REM sleep, which involves dreaming as well as a lighter form of non- REM sleep. Sleeping late is not good, as our bodies are not tailored to do so. For a very long time, human sleep patterns have been in sync with the daily variation in exposure to light. Our bodies are adapted to waking up in the morning and sleeping at night, not the other way around.

Many supplements can be used to induce sleep, including magnesium, which is affordable and easily accessible. Melatonin is another hormonal supplement that can be taken to improve sleep.

Be Patient

Patience is being able to endure tough times. It involves perseverance when provoked or under strain. Also, it means being able to keep your mind clear when needed. Patience is a major component of success, and for one to master it, it requires a certain effort. When you are patient, you:

- Become better at making decisions - you always take time to asses each and every situation, and you understand that rushing into decisions is not wise. As you learn the benefits of being patient, you have fewer chances of making mistakes. When you are patient, you have more power. In short, patience is about acting at the right time.

- Become less stressed - you understand that some things take time, and waiting for them to take place is not bad. When you are patient, you are less likely to be stressed, angry, or overwhelmed.

- Will be better at relationships - when you have patience, you will be more flexible and understanding of others' mistakes, as well as their weaknesses. Also, you will be able to build stronger and longer-lasting relationships. Patience and perseverance can magically make difficulties disappear, and obstacles vanish.

To be able to solve life's problems, you need to understand them fully. This is why you need to learn to be patient. Your patience originates from your childhood. The way you cope in life is not any different from how you used to as a child. If you had a habit of throwing tantrums so that your parents could let you have your way, then your initial level of patience was low.

On the contrary, if you had parents that were strict but encouraging, you are likely to have developed a different character and coped well with problems. This means that your initial level of patience was high.

Patience is not something that comes overnight. You need to know that:

- Patience has to be developed over time.

- Patience is built by patience.

- Understand and counteract your triggers.

Impatience is something that is triggered; it doesn't just happen on its own. The triggers vary from person to person, so you need to understand what your trigger is. Once you know what it is and feel the trigger building up, you can do exercises or carry out techniques to calm you down.

Have Self-Confidence

When one feels down, in loss of control, or overwhelmed, impatience kicks in. You may want something to happen immediately, but you don't seem to be able to do anything to speed things up. A person with self-confidence accepts situations as they are; he does not fight it but rather works with it. Patience and confidence go hand in hand.

Be Positive

To avoid having a negative outlook, concentrate on the positive things in life. By doing this, you will reduce tension and become happier. It is good always to turn a negative situation into a positive one.

Change Your Attitude

Understand that even if something happens later than expected, it's not a big deal; it will get done, and everything will be okay.

Visualize

Anticipate the expected problem and figure out how you will deal with it.

Relieve Tension and Stress

Being impatient is the release of accumulated stress and anxiety, so always try to release this stress to clean up your system.

Tips for Building Patience

- Select a day where you make patience your goal.

Make an effort to take your time and think about everything you do. When the day ends, observe all the wise decisions you made and what you understood from them. Patience is similar to physical activity because it requires persistence and effort.

- Take your time.

If you find yourself rushing to try to get things done in a hurry, stop. Before acting, take several deep breaths. Being impatient does not make things move faster in any way.

- Practice delayed gratification.

Whenever you want to buy something, stop and think first! Perhaps you don't need it as much as you think and can save money by avoiding to buy on impulse.

- Think before talking.

At times, we talk without thinking about the consequences of our words. Pause and go over what you want to say before you do to avoid hurting or offending other people.

Patience is a must when attempting to lose weight, attaining goals, having a baby, working out, excelling in your career, as well as many other situations that you will face in life. It is a valuable trait to nurture. It may seem passive, but it is actually a form of self-discipline.

Chapter 4: Clear Your Mind

Clear thinking has been defined as not being confused and having the ability to think clearly and intelligently or being clear-headed. In my view, clear thinking is having the presence of mind to manage your thoughts effectively, analyze them, and ultimately make sound decisions.

To be a clear thinker, you need the ability to process thoughts in detail through independent and introspective thinking. It is more than the acquisition of information as it is not singularly dependent on memory - you must be capable of preventing consequences for greater knowledge and sound decisions.

Moreover, clear thinking entails much more than the act of thinking itself and involves mental nurturing, health, and the shaping of our lives. Our thinking or thoughts essentially determine who we turn out to be; you make decisions every day with far-reaching consequences, all from the same source - the mind. Therefore, mental health and clarity are key to making good decisions.

De-Clutter the Mind

Clear thinking requires clear thoughts. A mind that is cluttered is on edge and distracted, and in this state, you are not focused, and very little is achieved.

The following are ways to free up your brain and de-clutter your mind:

Write It Down

There is a lot that goes on in your brain, and you do not need to store everything in there. Instead, write everything down. This can be anything that allows you to put down a piece of information that you do not want to forget. For example, if you have an appointment or any future projects with important deadlines, have it diarized or marked it your calendar. It is also advisable to keep a journal, which is more detailed. A journal will help you offload anything that keeps you from getting things done like relationship problems, giving you peace of mind.

Discard Memories of the Past

Memories that are filled with mistakes, people we have wronged, past failures, as well as missed opportunities, should be let go. Most people usually hold on to these memories and refuse to move past them. Memories that bring you down litter your mind and your life and cloud your mind from clear thinking.

Avoid Multi-Tasking

When you decide to take on tasks, start by choosing the most important one and work down until the last is tackled. Also, do not take on more than one task at a time. Devote a specific amount of time to organize everything.

During that time, ensure that your mind is clear and push anything that can distract you from the task at hand aside.

Control the Amount of Information You Take In

Too much information can choke up your brain. You must control the information that you take in every day from magazines, newspapers, TV, as well as social media and the internet.

Limit the amount of information you take in by setting a specific time to spend on social media and other sources of information. Unsubscribe from online magazines and blogs that do not add any value to your life. Take opinions from individuals you hold in high regard and ignore irrelevant information.

Have a Routine

Have a routine for every aspect of your life and everything you do, as this will greatly help reduce stress. Even simple things like what to eat for breakfast, lunch, and supper, as well as what to wear every day, need to be scheduled and prepared in advance.

Prioritize

There are quite a number of things that you need to do on a daily basis. However, you cannot do everything; have a list of important things and deal with those first. It gives your mind time and space for mental clarity.

Mental clutter leads to the obstruction of our inner thoughts and gets in the way of clear thinking and what is really important. Begin clearing your mind of all the unnecessary things that take up space in your mind but do not add any value or enhance clear thinking.

Bedtime Solutions

There is nothing more important for the proper functioning of the brain than good rest. Getting enough quality sleep is the best way to enhance clear thinking.

Getting enough sleep helps in the protection and enhancement of your health - both mental and physical, as well as the safety and quality of your life. Good sleeping habits will ensure that you are protected health-wise, both mentally and physically, and ensure that you are safe in your day to day activities.

Sleep offers the brain time to rest, be refreshed, and get much-needed rejuvenation after a long day of activity. A rested and relaxed mind is a great reservoir and resource for clear thinking and well-grounded decisions.

Many of us underestimate the power of getting enough sleep, but according to research, sleep is very important because:

- It helps your brain to function and to work properly. When you sleep, your brain gets to rest and rejuvenate to help you learn and remember information; a good night's sleep improves learning, helps to better pay attention, as well as in decision making and creativity.

- It helps maintain a healthy body balance of hormones, enabling proper body function.

- Sleeping well and at the right time helps you function properly throughout the day, as your mind is rejuvenated, allowing you to be more productive.

People who are sleep deficient are generally less productive, take longer to finish tasks, have a slower reaction time, and make more mistakes. Therefore, the simple remedy to the mistakes you commit and the cure for lower productivity is getting enough quality sleep.

Tips for a Good Night's Sleep

- Exercise - exercise regularly by going on walks, jogs, or any other form of physical activity before the day ends.

- Skipping the nap - avoid sleeping in the afternoon since afternoon naps can lead to nighttime insomnia.

- If you can't sleep, the best thing to do is get out of bed and do something relaxing until you feel like sleeping again.

- Limit caffeine and alcohol intake close to bedtime since they are common causes of sleep deficiency.

- Avoid watching TV until late as some programs may be so stimulating that they result in poor or insufficient sleep.

- Observe good sleeping hygiene, which includes using your bedroom primarily to sleep and sticking to a regular sleep schedule.

Sleep and clear thinking are inseparable. Why should you pay money to see a doctor when a good night's sleep can be the cure?

The above tips will ensure that you get enough sleep for a refreshed and clear mind. A good night's rest will improve your efficiency, and more importantly, improve your performance and ability to have clear thinking.

Get enough sleep, get your brain, have your mind rested, and wake up with the mental lucidity you need for everyday decision-making and thought-processing. Sleep is the spa of the brain and the natural way your mind gets to relax and heal from the rigors of daily activity.

Avoid Alcohol — It Is the Last Thing Your Brain Needs

A clear brain thinks, well, clearly. Mental clarity is critical and essential to managing your thoughts effectively.

The brain is responsible for thought processing and decision-making; hence, for it to function optimally, it is, therefore, imperative that you keep it healthy. When your brain is clouded or fatigued by any stimuli, you will not have a clear mind, and one such substance is alcohol.

Alcohol has the ability to shape your thinking and feelings, effectively influencing the way you think. When one consumes alcohol, they cannot think clearly because the brain functioning is diminished and does not work swiftly or efficiently. If you look at someone who is drunk, you will notice they have slow impulses, are clumsy, have vague speech, and talk a lot, so it is obvious that alcohol affects the brain in some way.

Short-term exposure to alcohol leads to a hazy brain; the person who is under the influence stops being concerned, worried, and anxious. Medium-term exposure to alcohol does result in mood swings and apprehension, which is only eased by consuming more alcohol. Long-term exposure can lead to severe depression and dementia.

Alcohol affects a person in three ways; however, the effects vary by person, depending on size, gender, how much and how fast you drink, and your previous experience with alcohol.

Affects Feeling

Your feelings will be determined by your blood alcohol concentration. You may feel stimulated because alcohol reduces shyness, or your reflexes may be impaired, and you may become noisy and violent. The more booze you take in, the more it influences how you feel.

Affects Actions

Alcohol will affect how you behave. You may become more confident, making it easier to socialize with others. Some make unwise decisions when drunk; for example, they may decide to engage in sex or take drugs when they are intoxicated because alcohol inhibits clear thinking.

Affects the Body System

Alcohol travels through the bloodstream and alters the blood supply in various parts of the body. When temperatures fall, someone under the influence of alcohol misleadingly feels warmer, putting them at risk of hypothermia.

The liver metabolizes alcohol to eradicate it from the body. It takes the liver one hour to break down the alcohol in one drink, so if you overstrain the liver with too much alcohol, it will not perform optimally. Furthermore, consuming too much alcohol in a short period of time may put you in a coma; you stop breathing because alcohol is a depressant that reduces the pulse and breathing rate.

A lack of mental clarity leads to hasty and poor decisions that are not well thought through, and that will most certainly lead to bad results. Over time, excessive consumption of alcohol leads to diminished reasoning and thinking capacity.

The ability to think clearly is critical in order to be able to function efficiently and make sound decisions. When you consume too much alcohol, mental clarity is greatly hampered. To master the art of clear thinking, you must control your alcohol intake or stop drinking altogether. It is especially important to avoid making any critical decisions when under the influence. Just wait until you are sober.

While modest amounts of alcohol can be lead to creative thinking, research shows that it is bad for your brain's long-term health. Drink to unwind, not to think, and drink modestly.

Nurture Your Artistic Side

Have you ever experienced a feeling that makes your mind a mess of thoughts, and you are not sure what to do next? This feeling is fairly common in a world with numerous responsibilities.

The arts are a good source of mental creativity and can be quite helpful in managing your thought process. Visual creative arts like writing and drawing can especially be of great assistance in the pursuit of clear thinking.

Writing is cathartic and has been proven to help coordinate your thoughts; basically, it helps to unlock space for your thoughts to breathe. Churning out three handwritten articles every day can de-clutter your thoughts and clear your mind.

To achieve clear thinking through writing, record how you feel, why you are feeling that way, and what you think you want to do about it. You will then be able to look at what you have written down, reflect on it, and get a feeling of accomplishment.

This trick usually helps to literally throw your thoughts away—write what you think is disturbing you, crumble the paper and throw it away. According to research, people who throw away the concerns they have written down on paper are less likely to be bothered by them.

You can also express your feelings through drawing, as drawing is a powerful tool that will help you clear your thoughts. You do not have to be an amazing artist. All you need is a piece of paper and a pencil or crayons.

Here are some benefits of nurturing your artistic side:

Art Stimulates Creative Thinking

Whether you are writing free-form or a novel, the act of writing keeps your artistic juices flowing. You are able to connect logically between thoughts, new ideas emerge, and you end up being creative.

Writing also makes you take ideas out of your head and put them down in writing. It challenges you to think of how you can relay that information to your readers in a way that makes sense.

Creative Art Reduces Stress

When you are totally immersed in 'the artistic zone,' you get clarity of mind. This meditative state puts your mind at ease; activities like drawing and painting are soothing and fulfilling hobbies that can lower your stress levels and leave you feeling mentally calm and clear.

Art also provides a distraction, giving your brain a break from negative thoughts. According to Leonardo da Vinci, painting embraces the ten functions of the eye; light and darkness, location and shape, color and body, closeness and distance, and motion and rest.

Boosts Self-Esteem and Bestows a Sense of Accomplishment

Art enhances your drive, concentration, and focus. It enables you to plan for the future and defy impulses to be able to accomplish your goals. Creative art enables your hormones to transmit dopamine, also known as the 'motivation molecule,' which fuels the creation of neurons and alerts the brain for learning.

Writing and drawing have been proven to be highly effective ways to enhance clear thinking. You do not have to be an accomplished artist or writer; if you feel stressed or that your mind is a mess, all you need to do is take a piece of paper and put down your thoughts through writing or drawing.

How Clean Is Your Environment?

Clear thinking requires a clean environment, so if you are surrounded by disorder, you will constantly be distracted and won't be able to think clearly because of the mess you are wallowing in. When your surrounding is untidy, the mess blocks your ability to focus and interferes with your brain's ability to process information optimally. So, your attention is now divided between clutter and mental clarity.

It is important to organize your space and make it appealing and ideal for good and lucid thought processing. You may not know it, but if your surrounding is a mess, your mental balance is affected, as your disgust and concerns about the tidiness of your space will be a distraction to clear thinking.

Clear all the mess around your office, on your desk, in your house, or your closet, which is a result of you not arranging or putting your stuff in order.

Clean regularly; set aside a day and time every week to clean, arrange, and get your office or house in order. Get rid of items that you do not need like clothes you no longer wear and clear your desk of all the papers that are no longer useful.

Avoid placing things where they do not belong; once a single item is in the wrong place, you are on your way to a messy road. Repeated actions become habits, and habits are really hard to kick, so do not get in the habit of throwing things around and causing a mess.

Organized people regularly get rid of things that they no longer need to create more room for them and avoid the mess that comes with piling up unnecessary items to achieve a serene surrounding conducive to creativity.

Below are a few pointers to keep your surroundings clean to enable you to think clearly and boost your productivity:

Clear the Surfaces

Get rid of all unwanted items on your desk, tables, and floor. Once the surfaces are cleared, the mess is virtually gone, leaving you less distracted with a relaxed mind that is suited for clear thinking.

Manage Your Waste Paper

There is nothing as messy as waste paper, so you need to get rid of it as soon as it appears. DO NOT print something unless you have to, and even then, proofread it and make sure the content is right to avoid needing to re-print.

Cancel all the subscriptions that you don't need so that they don't pile up in your office or home.

Manage Digital Clutter

Get into a daily or weekly routine of clearing your email and social accounts of all junk and mail that you've already read.

An overflowing email account can be very stressful and distracting to thinking clearly and being productive. Organize and manage your digital documents into folders for easier access. If it's really necessary, invest in a digital document management system.

Clear every aspect of your life of things that you no longer need, and you will lead a much better, more organized life with clear thinking.

Get Your Blood Pumping

One of the best and easiest ways to achieve mental relaxation and clear thinking is by exercising regularly. The benefits of regular physical exercise to the body and mind for overall good health are enormous.

Physical exercise contributes greatly to reduced stress by enabling a state of mental and physical calmness and serenity, freeing you from mental tension and persistent anxiety. Mental calmness is the ideal condition for good thought processing and clear thinking.

The best exercises for mental relief and relaxation are aerobic exercises like running, skipping, jogging, and cycling—all of which are great for your health. These will lift your mood, boost your energy, heighten your concentration, as well as focus and relax your body and mind. By sweating, the body gets to get rid of underlying tension by working the muscles and releasing beneficial body hormones, which help the brain relax.

Exercise also supports other areas of general health; for example, those who exercise regularly get better sleep as they are more relaxed and are likely to have better cardiovascular health. Good physical health is critical for mental clarity and clear thinking; when you are physically unwell, you lack the mental capacity for clear thinking due to the distraction of the illness you are suffering or recovering from.

You do not have to be in a gym to exercise; you can exercise almost anywhere with enough space. If you feel bogged down by stress or mental fatigue, simply walk around or jog in your place to get your blood pumping. This will allow good chemicals like endorphins to flow through your body to boost your feelings and make you happy.

Apart from boosting your mood, exercise makes you mentally and physically stronger, which enables you to confront mental pressure more comfortably. Susceptibility to illnesses and stress is greatly reduced if you exercise regularly, leaving you fully healthy in body and mind.

If you have been feeling the pressures of work and have not been able to figure out how to deal with the stress, try exercising, and you will be surprised at how much better you feel. Exercising allows the release of feel-good brain hormones that fend off diseases that affect memory like Alzheimer's- a degenerative disease that affects the brain and mental health.

Exercise and relaxation are guaranteed to be able to help you deal with mental stress and boost your mental health and clarity. Make sure to take up exercises that are not too vigorous for you- do your research and talk to experts before settling on the right exercise regime for you.

Therefore, being physically active will help you think clearly, reduce stress, and lead to a healthier, happier life. Start now by doing light exercises before embarking on more vigorous routines, and you will be left wondering why you did not start exercising sooner. More importantly, you will reap the benefits and achieve the ability to think clearly.

The Magic of Melody

Music is good for the mind thanks to its relaxing qualities and its ability to enhance the processing of information; it has been proven that musicians' cerebellums are bigger and that they have more grey matter than regular people.

The use of music to help with thinking is a proven technique that works; through certain melodies and musical pitches, the brain tends to be more active and better at processing information, and this is how music helps for clear thinking.

By affecting and influencing our feelings and emotions, music can influence our thinking and determine our decisions. Music also improves and boosts creativity - soothing melodies catalyze creativity and clear thinking by stimulating positive hormones. However, to achieve optimal music-induced creativity and clear thinking, the music has to be played at low volume, as loud music is distractive to clear thought processing and thinking.

Studies have shown that music improves our motor skills and reasoning, thereby improving our understanding, enhancing our ability to analyze information, and effectively discerning things. These are the exact traits you for you to master the art of clear thinking.

Music has an indisputable ability to lift our moods. If, for example, you were struggling to come up with a solution on a project you were working on, just take some time off work, play some of your favorite soothing music and get back to cracking the problem- you will be surprised at how much better and faster you will be able to solve it.

Music in general and classical pieces, in particular, have the ability to activate the left and right sides of the brain, in effect enabling better learning and information retention. When you listen to soothing music, neurons that relax the brain are released, allowing optimal performance.

Slow music also has another great effect on the body, which is healthy for the mind and the ability to think clearly. Slow music will slow the heart rate and breathing, thus lowering the blood pressure for better health.

The positive power and effect of music on our thought processing and clarity of mind cannot be questioned; it is now up to you to harness these same benefits in your favor to be able to attain the ability for clear thinking. Research and studies on students who listened to and played music found that they were better academic performers; their audio capabilities were better; they retained information better, had higher memory capabilities, and performed better than those who had no consistent or regular association with music.

Start listening to good soothing music for mental clarity; you can set aside a time during the day for you to listen to these melodies to relax from the stresses of the day. Listen to music in the evening before you go to bed, or you may even decide to learn to play a musical instrument. During these moments, allow no distractions to reap the profound benefits of clear thinking through the power of music.

Do It Now!

Procrastination is a big hindrance to clear thinking; if you keep pushing aside decision making, you will be faced with an overflow of information that you will not be able to keep up with. Handling things as they come eases your mind and helps you think clearly.

Life is full of decisions to be made, and they do not stop because you are unable to settle on something. We make decisions all the time—picking what outfit to wear, where to eat, etc.

Making quick decisions is valuable since it will save you time and energy. Even though decisions are dictated by the weight of the problem or situation, it is important to know that taking too much time to reach a decision can cause more harm than good.

Many of us fail to make quick decisions because we fear to be wrong; however, this delaying only further weighs on our minds and clouds our thoughts. A worried mind has no clarity whatsoever and cannot be relied upon for sound decisions. The inability to reach quick decisions is also referred to as analysis paralysis.

You can overcome indecisiveness by using the following tips to help with your decision-making process:

Learning to Trust Your Intuition

Trust your instinct and make decisions based on the three forms of intuition. Ordinary intuition is the basic normal feeling you have about something, expert intuition, of course, is based on gathered skills and experience, and the third strategic intuition is based on clear thought.

Leaning on Experience and Advice

Make decisions based on your past experience or someone else's experience. Reach out to somebody for help, or you can look back at a similar situation you faced in the past and use that experience.

Reasoning the Problem Out

Use the information available to you, as well as the facts and figures you have to help you settle on a decision. Reasoning a problem out should help you to quickly analyze the available facts and make a decision based on the particular fact that outweighs the others in that situation.

Importance of the Decision

Of what importance is the decision that you want to make? Depending on the magnitude of the decision, the time taken to decide will vary. For example, you cannot objectively settle on whom to marry and spend the rest of your life within a few hours-it will take longer than that, and conversely, you can't take a year to decide what to wear!

Fixing Your Priorities

Get organized and prioritize your decision making. Do not let yourself be swarmed by issues that you can quickly handle and get out of the way; clear your decision making by acting on the problems as they come and deciding on the simpler ones first.

Decision making can still be a tall order, despite the foregoing tips on how to be quicker at it. The following factors can slow down your decision making:

Lack of Sufficient Information

When you don't have enough information about a problem, you will naturally feel like your impending decision is wrong, as you are not adequately informed. Therefore, prior to decision making, you need to gather enough information.

Too Much Information

Too much information is a hurdle to fast decision making. If you have too much information, it will be difficult to decide which decision to take, leading to a higher likelihood of procrastinating.

Seeking the Input of Many People

Time is an important factor in decision making, and involving too many people can be a challenge as it leads to taking more time to decide. Different people will give you different opinions or options, which will eventually lead to confusion. Consult people you think have been in a situation like yours before and reach out to no more than three of them.

Avoiding Being Emotional

Being too emotional in your decision making can make the decision even harder to reach as emotions can make you irrational. So, when making important and quick decisions, keep your emotions in check.

Our brains have the capacity and capability to process information quickly; we just decide not to. Quick decisions can be very helpful, but I would still caution you against making hasty decisions, especially on critical matters.

Adopt these tips for a faster and more reliable decision making for clear thinking.

Get on the Move

One of the healthiest, cheapest, and easiest ways of clearing your mind for free thought, mental clarity, and relaxation is taking a walk. Walks or strolls are even more fulfilling and cathartic when done in a natural environment, surrounded by trees and the beautiful sounds of nature.

Walking combines the benefits of aerobics by pumping your heart and working your body out, leading to a mind free of worries for clear thinking. Experiments have confirmed that regularly walking can improve memory and focus by exercising the brain and cultivating mental rejuvenation by stimulating the growth of neurons. When you're walking, you have time for yourself and your thoughts, and you do not have to worry about your work assignments or any other troubles you may be facing.

A stroll will uplift your moods and influence you to think positively; since walking does not take much mental effort to accomplish, your brain is left with room to think freely and clearly. You also get to clear your mind of all distractions and think of fresh, new ideas. Most creative people have claimed that they got an idea or solved a lingering problem when walking - you are not any different, so start walking and reap the benefits of creativity and free thought.

Walking increases blood circulation and enhances oxygen exposure to the brain; a well-oxygenated brain is well-nourished and makes it think more clearly. Positive hormones are stimulated and released in the brain, and these hormones induce good positive thought and creative thinking.

After a walk, due to the release of mental tension and physical stress, your way of thinking, and cognitive skills are dramatically improved. Studies have confirmed that in the short and long term, walking exercises enhance memory and mental skills, essentially making you better at decision making and organizing your thoughts.

A sedentary life is not healthy either; walking exercises will keep you active and improve your overall health. Apart from reaping mental clarity, you will benefit from physical fitness, which will help you fend off unhealthy conditions like obesity and cardiovascular problems. Exercise keeps you active and alert - you will generally be in a good positive mood, which is a good place to cultivate clear thoughts.

If you walk regularly, you will be more creative, and your mind will be energized to spawn better ideas. Start walking today and reap the benefits of clear thinking that will lead to a more relaxed mind and better health.

Fewer Sweets Will Do It

If you have a sweet tooth, you have probably realized that when you consume sugar, you are usually mentally fatigued, nervous, and clouded. Sugar is not good for the brain and is detrimental to clear thinking.

Sugar is important for hormonal body balance; however, a high intake of refined sugar is not good for the entire body, and especially the brain, as it damages constituent cells. In fact, the brain reacts to too much sugar as it does with a virus or bacteria, resulting in diminished cognitive capabilities.

Sugar is not good for the mind since it is a stress activator. It stimulates stress hormones, which affect memory, thus limiting your mental clarity. It will slow down neural communication, as it interferes with brain synaptic activity and causes stress to the brain, leading to the destruction of brain cells.

Sugars in fizzy drinks such as sodas are even worse; they cause a sugar rush in your body, which triggers the pancreas to release a large quantity of insulin into the bloodstream, which is unhealthy and leaves you stressed and makes your mind clouded.

Try eating a sweet snack when you are hungry, wait for twenty minutes, and try to solve a mathematics problem to find out how bad sugar is to your mind. You will find that your mind is so fuzzy and unsteady that it is difficult to solve the problem. Sugar clouds the mind so much that it is actually considered a drug if taken in copious amounts.

By interfering with your cognitive abilities and memory, sugar essentially makes you less smart. Your intellect is diminished, resulting in a lower ability to think things through and reach good decisions.

My advice is that if you want to maintain a clear mind, keep your consumption of table sugar at a minimum level. Completely avoid sodas and other fizzy drinks, but if you really can't, consider them a treat that you can have once in a while when you do not need to handle any task that will require focused mental engagement. Anyway, drastically lower your intake of fizzy drinks so that you do not suffer its destructive effects.

Of course, apart from the direct, immediate effects of sugar, there are several health problems that go along with it. Many chronic diseases and conditions such as diabetes are caused by an unhealthy intake of sugar.

Additionally, the fats and calories converted from the sugar you are consuming will contribute to obesity and cardiovascular problems, which will obviously divert your attention and focus from the main goal of clear thinking. You will constantly be worrying about your health and how to get better, and the expenses that come with these conditions that can be avoided will also add to your stress and negatively impact your mental health.

For a clear mind, stay away from sugar or limit your sugar intake to healthy levels.

Chapter 5: Mental Strength

There is a lot of faulty and invalid information everywhere around this particular topic, both in the media and the outside. The major aim of this chapter is to demystify the popular myths about mental toughness — the how's and why's of mental toughness.

Myths About Mental Strength

First, here are some of the most common myths about mental strength:

Myth Number One: Mentally Strong People Don't Have Fears, Doubts, and Agitations

That is far from the truth! The idea that mental toughness implies that an individual never has tension or agitations is total BS. Fear, doubts, and tension are typical, sound human feelings. Hence, mentally tough individuals can and do encounter them just like any other person.

However, there is a difference in how mentally tough individuals handle their fear and tension, as they don't give fear and agitations a chance to meddle with their daily lives. At the end of the day, they figure out how to take their apprehensions and tension. They are curious to see what happens.

Truth be told, exceptional competitors and entertainers go a long way to realize how to utilize and manage nervousness; they train in order to use tension to further bolster their advantage in approaches that lead to ideal execution. Experts train themselves to get rid of their uneasiness through diligent work and commitment (that is how they became experts, after all!). If they can do it, you can do it too. This brings us to myth number two.

Myth Number Two: Mental Toughness Is Either Inborn or Not

Although there are many facts that point out that a few people normally have larger amounts of flexibility than others, it is absolutely false that resilience is a "win big or bust" attribute that an individual was either born with or not, like being born with blue eyes, for example. Life isn't a theory, nor is the situation of whether an individual is mentally tough or not. Just like other mental attributes, mental toughness is a skill that can be developed like a muscle; it works through deliberate preparation and experience. Believe me when I say it's achievable—I witness it consistently!

To perform at the optimal level under pressure, you must have the capability to "self-direct." When you develop the ability to perform effectively, at that stage, excellence performance becomes normal. Also, when you start performing effectively, at that point, you start to trust that you will keep performing effectively. This feeling of trust in yourself and that you are able to defeat misfortune given your present aptitudes, capacities, and information is referred to as "self-adequacy." It is one of the main highlights of mental toughness.

Continue learning and practicing self-control skills with the aim to effectively approach and conquer the challenges in your life instead of running away from them. A majority of people are amazed by the fact that having the certainty of approaching difficulties in life isn't really required. Confidence will definitely come later, but it doesn't necessarily have to be there to succeed. The skills, however, should be there.

Myth Number Three: Mentally Tough People Never Quit

Aspects of being a mentally tough individual include endurance, fortitude, and the willpower to push through in difficult situations. There is a tendency to be too dogged and passionate about some difficulties.

In training and competition, it is sometimes essential to give up. You can identify an amateur or an individual who is mentally rigid when they don't pull out of training when they should. They either don't know their boundaries, or they deliberately ignore it. When they cross those boundaries, athletes often get in trouble. There is usually a lot of pressure to remain steady in these circumstances because the rules never change or bend; therefore, giving up at this point is the wisest thing to do.

There is a knowledge that serves as a guideline to know the origin of the line. This information comes through guidance from expert trainers and therapists, as well as through personal experience and psychological symptoms experienced during practice and competition. Be watchful of your limits when training for a competition.

The major point to note in this complicated subject is to accept that, as competitors, a thin line exists where giving up is the best thing to do.

Myth Number Four: Mentally-Strong People Focus Solely on Victory and Results

All the outcomes in victories, disappointments, and losses have genuine ramifications. In reality, results truly matter. In any situation, if you want to enlarge your performance base and achieve a set goal, it is a very bad idea to focus squarely on the future result instead of concentrating on the occasion.

It doesn't mean that mentally tough individuals don't think optimistically or that they abstain from thinking of the future and setting objectives. Also, it doesn't mean that they don't use mental pictures as inspiration to achieve their objectives when competing and preparing for competition. It simply means that they never allow distracting thoughts about the future to cloud their minds, like focusing on how they will perform on a given day or whether they will win or lose. This act brings them out of their concentration on the present moment, and being aware of it is required for perfect execution.

Experts in the field, however, try to keep up the pace as much as possible and maintain undivided attention in what they are doing. They ceaselessly upgrade their mindfulness by continually moving between the big picture and significant subtleties inserted in the master plan. They continually analyze how their bodies are feeling, how they are positioned, and execute different ideas in relation to what they are doing.

It is extremely important to develop your mind to concentrate on the present moment, in training and competition, and in the process of execution. At that point, based on your input, the best result will take care of itself.

Myth Number Five: Mentally Tough People Are Usually Perfectionists

Perfectionism is a grueling attitude. There are two kinds of perfectionism: the beneficial and the hurtful one. The former is classified as the "perfectionist striving," and the latter is referred to as the "perfectionist concern," although this myth in itself is not totally accurate.

When the perfectionist strivers go through bitterness and setbacks, they do not dwell on it for too long. They are very meticulous about their next execution even after they allow themselves to mourn on their misfortune and disappointments.

As such, they accumulate whatever information they need to proceed, they store and apply it, and after that, shift their concentration to whatever the next task is.

As opposed to the self-versus-other focus of perfectionistic concerns, the strivers have a self-oriented point of view that includes concentrating on one's process (e.g., "Am I better, more grounded, and more self-caring than I was yesterday?") as opposed to those of others. As you may effectively guess, a perfectionistic striving view is directly related to a high rate of focus and performance as well as self-compassion, pressure, and better physical well-being.

Myth Number Six: Misfortunes Are Unfavorable to Developing Mental Toughness

Every dilemma and difficulty brings with it the opportunity to grow and become a better individual. When crises and trials hit us squarely in the face, we often neglect the myriad of opportunities that they bring and forget to use that avenue for our personal growth and for more flexibility.

When you are confident enough to take risks in one aspect of your life (for instance, your physical well-being), the flexibility you develop in that area will influence you in other aspects (for instance, in your social interactions). Simply focus on acquiring skills from experts who can guide you instead of fretting or worrying about a lack of confidence.

A major feature of misfortunes and trials is the maintenance of mental alertness and the development of new ways of endurance. Hardships, discomfort, worries, and doubts help an individual. Without adversity, we would neither grow nor become stronger, so do not run away from a challenge but try rather dealing with it in a modest way.

Things That Mentally Strong People Never Do

It is possible for you to work hard and smart, but it would be unnecessary for you to add more habits to your hectic lifestyle in order for you to attain your peak potential. You can be smart as well as effective at work by reducing the patterns that eliminate efficiency and reduce mental strength.

The following are thirteen major things that mentally strong people do *not* engage in:

Self-Pity

Giving room for pity parties in difficult situations only expands problems and complicates matters. Even if you are going through a particular illness or you can't meet up with your bills, it's a total waste of time to throw pity parties and to indulge in your inadequacies, disappointments by exaggerating your tragedies and keeping track records of all the difficulties you have endured.

Regardless of the crisis or challenge, you can choose to have a positive mental attitude and not give in to pity parties because they never offer solutions to your problems; it only escalates the difficulty. Be grateful for three key things in your life to keep self-pity at bay.

Giving Away Their Ability

If you constantly feel like a victim, it's impossible for you to be mentally vigorous. Nobody can control your life except yourself, with your thoughts and actions. In other words, if you allow other people's actions to rule your life and emotions, you indirectly give them the power to direct your life.

The factors that influence your daily decisions can be seen in your speech. For instance, instead of saying, "I think I need to work for extra hours today," say, "I'm going to stay late." There might be consequences to not working late, but it's still a choice. Self-empowerment is fundamental to create the sort of life you want.

Running Away from Change

We are in a world where things are constantly evolving, and your success largely depends on your ability to fit in. If you don't want to stay stuck in the old way doing things, don't worry about change complicating things.

If you consistently practice handling stress from various angles, you will become much more confident in your ability to adjust to any situation, such as walking away from a toxic relationship, starting a new job, and so on.

Wasting Their Mental Effort and Energy on Things They Have No Power to Regulate

It is better to invest your mental and physical energy on solving problems rather than on wishful thinking and grumbling. Doing this will allow you to be ready for whatever circumstance comes your way.

When you notice that you are about to slip into depression mode because of things you can't control, such as the attitude of other people and the choices they make, you should channel that energy toward a worthwhile cause. You could help a colleague get their work done or complete an unfinished project you have at hand. You have to learn to deal with conditions that you can't control and concentrate on influencing people rather than bossing them around.

Worrying About Pleasing Everyone

You can't possibly make everyone happy, and if you try to, you might get burned out mentally, and you will most likely miss your goals. Regardless of what the situation might be, whether your father-in-law dislikes you or you are forced to go to a ceremony you don't want to attend, you can't please everyone.

Before you can live a genuine life, you have to set rules according to your own standards, and sometimes, you will make choices that annoy others. Concentrate solely on utilizing your energy for your top five values and stay committed to achieving them.

Fear of Taking Risks

When you are enthusiastic about a new adventure, you are not afraid to take a giant leap of faith and face it head-on. If you are scared, it might be difficult for you to take any crucial steps.

Extraordinary people are individuals who are not afraid of taking chances, and your emotions can rob you of clear critical thinking, stopping you from taking intelligent risks. It's vital for you to make a detailed list of the advantages and disadvantages of making a decision based on accurate logic and emotions. Recognize your feelings and determine how your emotions can influence your thoughts.

Living in the Past

When you habitually dwell on the memories of the past, it could damage you emotionally. Although it is essential to gain lessons from our past experiences, we must not dwell on it to the point that it breaks us emotionally. Learn to let go of the past.

You can ask questions about the past once in a while, but it shouldn't keep you from focusing on the present and creating a beautiful future. When you let go of the past, you do away with emotional baggage, such as non-forgiveness, bitterness, anger, and every other kind of negative emotion. Develop yourself through hurtful situations rather than reliving the past all over again.

Repeating Other People's Failures

Whenever you fail, it is an opportunity to learn and be a better person. Perhaps you recovered the weight that you promised yourself you wouldn't, or you overlooked a vital due date. Perhaps you felt embarrassed when you gave the wrong answer in class, or you were made fun of for failing an exam. Since a young age, you have been conditioned to believe that mistakes are awful.

You may hide or excuse your mistakes to cover the disgrace and embarrassment, but doing so will keep you from learning from them. Look at every failure as a greater opportunity for development. Be honest with yourself and assess why you failed.

Being Jealous of Other People's Achievement

Jealousy is a dangerous attitude. When you watch a colleague get promoted or receive an award, or when you overhear your neighbor talking about their latest house, what goes on in your mind? Envy or gratitude?

Therefore, you have the power to make the law work for you, knowingly or unknowingly. Either way, it is happening, so you are better off making it work for you in a positive way by adopting the correct principles and taking the right steps to achieve the right mindset. Because this law of attraction is always in existence, let us then learn how to harness its power for a more wholesome, better life.

Quitting Upon the First Loss

Have you ever thought about Thomas Edison's failure? You might not have known this, but Edison made hundreds of attempts before he finally invented the functioning light bulb we make use of today. Almost every true success story started with tons of failed attempts before eventually getting it right.

Do not be the kind of person who avoids failure because of the fear of defeat. Steer clear of your comfort zone and venture into the limitations. Even if you don't win in your first attempt and people embarrass and insult you, keep at it. Don't look back and keep improving yourself till the point of expertise. Stay determined in your pursuit of self-improvement. Keep trying again, and again, and again.

The Fear of Solitude

A lot of people are scared by the thought of being alone in the comfort of their musings. Solitude can either be effective or ineffective. It's a beneficial habit for you to have around ten minutes a day to be alone with your thoughts. However, many people run away from silence due to their numerous activities and hectic work schedules.

A Feeling of Entitlement to the World

It's a very poor mindset to wait for people to give you what you want as a result of your hard work and effort. Sometimes, we feel too entitled to success when we think we have done exceptionally well, sailing through the good times and the bad times. It is better for you to deliberately focus on everything you have to offer rather than what you think you deserve. No matter how you feel or think about the way life has treated you, you definitely have a value to offer.

Anticipating Speedy Results

Regardless of whether you're trying to reduce your tendencies to procrastinate or improve your marriage, expecting momentary results is delusional. Self-development is a gradual process. Learn to see obstacles as unimportant events and see your endeavors as a marathon and not a sprint.

Mental strength gives you the ability to scale through difficult times. You definitely require a lot of mental energy when life hits you in the face — like when facing the death of a friend, financial hardship, or a serious medical issue. Pay more attention to aspects in which you are doing great and take the opportunity to improve on whatever you need to. Everyone can develop his or her mental capacity. Work on being your very own mental strength mentor.

Make opportunities for development and, afterward, push yourself to become a little better today than you were yesterday. Mental toughness gives you the capability to observe the shortcomings of life and the temporary nature of a mortal man and accept the effects, which include worrying, doubts, fears, and uncertainties. This requires a blend of flexibility and willpower.

The world we live in is in disorder, and our lives are delicate and unpredictable. We are fully conscious of this fact, and in the absence of fear, we are ready to overcome the universe and overcome all odds.

Be committed to your goals until you get to the finish line.

Chapter 6: Law of Attraction

You may have been told this before, but I will repeat it again. Success is all about your mindset—the person with the right mindset will get what they want, while those with a fickle mental attitude will almost always fail. In essence, our thoughts determine whether we will succeed at something or not—you basically have the power to decide what direction to go and how high your achievements are going to be. I will give you great insights to follow for *wholesome* success by setting your mind right.

When you have the right mindset for success and, thus, the ability to control your thoughts, you allow yourself only to have thoughts that will allow clear, undistracted thinking to be in tune with your desire for success. When it comes to mind control, we all have the Law of Attraction at our disposal; basically, the premise of the law is that you will attract what you think. Think positively, and your life will take a positive trajectory, but think negatively, and you will inevitably invite doom and gloom to your life.

We will look at how you can set your mind right in every aspect of your life; work, personal, spiritual, or even wealth building by using the powerful ideas and principles of the Law of Attraction. Do you want the mental clarity, strength, and focus required to achieve success? You will learn how to begin on the path to mastering the law by looking at examples of famous people who have used the principles to great success, and we will go through a list of ideas, steps, and tips for your success.

I will introduce you to the process of setting your mind right for success by putting the Law of Attraction in action. Remember—there is no success in this world that is not orchestrated; it is purposed, planned, actioned, then realized. Success never happens by accident.

It begins here, and I hope you trust and believe that you have the ability to do it. Enjoy reading and learning inspirational insights to get in the right frame of mind for wholesome success.

The term was originated in the early 1900s by William Atkinson when he authored and published a book that mentioned the Law of Attraction in the title to propagate his idea of a new way of thinking. Atkinson introduced us to the concepts of using thought, inner energy, vibration, and more profound manifestations to attain the right mindset for success and happiness.

In his book, he was the first to explore the importance of the power of love in realizing desires, which is essentially the foundation of the law—basically, you must love something hard enough to get it.

What Is the Law of Attraction?

My understanding of the Law of Attraction is the modern filtered definition, which is simply that like attracts and manifests like. Positive thoughts attract and spawn positive things, and negative thoughts attract negativity.

So, to dissect it further and simplify it, the Law of Attraction is about actively directing and controlling your thoughts to achieve the right mindset for success and manifestations. The same is true for the negative things that you confront in your life; you are attracting them to you, usually unconsciously, but you have no idea you are doing it! Consider this benign example:

"I wonder why I can't get this promotion." When you think like this, you are already negative in your approach to the promotion you are seeking. The statement exhibits doubt and is already negative — "can't." These kinds of statements that we throw around all the time serve to attract negative energy and leave us with a defeatist mentality, which is a totally wrong mindset for success.

The point is that we are what we think; our thoughts mold us into who we are and shape the trajectory of our lives, whether upwards or downwards. This law is one of the numerous universal laws that govern the way we live, regardless of our geographical location, creed, or race—the law applies the same to all, as each and every one of us has the power to navigate the law to our advantage or detriment.

Therefore, you have the power to make the law work for you, knowingly or unknowingly. Either way, it is happening, so you are better off making it work for you in a positive way by adopting the correct principles and taking the right steps to achieve the right mindset. Because this law of attraction is always in existence, let us then learn how to harness its power for a more wholesome, better life.

How and where do we begin in our pursuit for the right mindset?

Getting Started on the Path to Success

The Law of Attraction can be very daunting and difficult to grasp when you are first introduced to it, so you may find it confusing and elusive. However, it doesn't have to turn out this way, as we will discuss a series of steps for you to take to help ease you into this great rhythm of mastering the law on your way to wholesome success.

It is also important to remember that the Law of Attraction is not just about material success or amassing wealth, as the law can be used to achieve success in every aspect of your life.

I want you to take these steps with the full knowledge and belief that the law will work for you in all areas of your life: career, weight loss, marriage, academics, and everything else you can think of. Work on your mindset, and then adopt the great ideas for the success you are longing for.

The following action steps can assist you in getting started:

Clear Your Thoughts and Clarify What You Want

You already know the power of your thoughts and how they manifest into what you eventually become - you are what you think. The first step in getting the right mindset for success is purifying your mind to clear your thoughts.

Train your mind to think positively and clear your thoughts of all negativity so that you realize the success you want to achieve. Clarity of mind and the control of thoughts require you to be actively aware of what you want and the direction of thought you want your mind to take.

It is important to start small, since changing ideas and beliefs that you have held and instilled in you for a long time is easy; it is not just your thoughts you are working on but your whole mindset. As you are working on mental clarity, clarify exactly what you want in your life by writing it down on paper.

Of course, as we are human, we cannot completely do away with negative thoughts, because sooner or later we are bound to have them. The trick is to know how to push aside or circumvent the negative thoughts so that you do not nurture them to manifest negative outcomes in your life.

Remember that your most dominant thoughts will manifest more in your life.

Put Out a Request and Let Your Feelings Work for You

Once you are sure of what you want, you need to request it by asking verbally and putting it down on paper. For example, say, "I want to own my house within two years," and write it down on your journal.

Then, use the positive thoughts you are now learning to generate to spawn positive feelings and emotions, as positive vibrations from your upbeat feelings will attract positive results.

Meditation and visualization is a good way to start; take about five to ten minutes at the beginning of the day to meditate on something you want in your life. Close your eyes and visualize that you possess it and are using it; conjure up feelings of happiness and thankfulness and affirm ownership.

To further help you with really feeling the life you want, you can create a vision chart in a journal or on your wall or computer screen to assist you in staying focused and to help your thoughts stay on the goal. You can use constant reminders—pin these vision reminders on your mirror, on your office cubicle, or any other personal space that you are sure to visit daily to help keep your mind focused on your goal.

Visualizing is so powerful that even doing it for a minute every day will lead to amazing results.

Act and Act It Out

These are two completely different things, and you need to understand these points very clearly.

To act is to work for or to work towards what you want, so do not make your wish or request and then hope for a miracle! The Law of Attraction is not about luck; if you want to be a lawyer, do everything you need to get you there - go to Law School, work to get the money for the schooling fees, pursue a scholarship, etc. Keep in mind that faith without action is dead.

Acting out is playing the role you are attracting. Now that your thoughts are clear and you have the feelings and affirmation of ownership, you must act like you have attracted the life and success that you want.

Imagine how you would feel and act if you had what you are attracting and replicate those feelings into your daily life and routine. Throw the worrying and anxiety out the window and start acting with confidence, happiness, joy, and gratefulness.

In essence, I am asking you to pretend that you already have the house, the car, the money, the vacation, the healing, etc. Act like you already have it, and it will come to you even faster.

Maybe you've heard of this technique before, but we're going to put a slightly different spin on it. One of the most effective steps you can do when working with the Law of Attraction is to BE the person who already has what you want. Imagine how you would feel if you already had whatever it is that you're trying to attract.

Fully Utilizing the Law

Your vibrations must match the vibrations of the universe from whom you expect the gift you requested and what you want to attract; in other words, the principles of the law must now be your normal behavior.

You must create, maintain and sustain the mental and emotional state to match the one you will be in once you get what you want; if you are seeking wealth, and then be wealthy in thought and action before you even get the money. Manifest abundance and wealth and let out feelings of lack and doubt, and be very grateful for what you already have; dress the part, talk the part, seek the life, think it, feel it, and declare that you are living it already.

Ten Ideas to Help You Master the Law of Attraction

For you to harness the immense power of the Law of Attraction, you must lead a certain kind of life, with certain predetermined ideas for you to achieve the result that awaits you at the end of your journey.

Setting your mind right for success is a pursuit; it is something that you go after as it will never come to you. Never! In this chapter, we will learn the steps and ideas to implement to allow you to have the necessary thoughts to set your mind right.

The following are steps you can take to attain the right mindset for success with the use of the Law of Attraction:

Decide What You Want, and Once You Decide, DO NOT Doubt the Decision

It is vital that you remember that you are dealing with the Law of Attraction and making requests through your thoughts. You must decide what you want, and once you have settled for something, do not second guess or doubt yourself.

Doubt is the genesis of bad negative thoughts and the antithesis of creative thoughts that lead to success; be clear and definite because if you send the wrong signals, you might attract unwanted results.

Write Down Your Desires or Wants

When you want anything, it is important that you write it down on a piece of paper; putting your thoughts down on paper is the first step to owning what you want. By writing your desires down, you have taken the first step in turning your thoughts and mental images into reality- you have already started creating!

While writing, you should always start off with gratitude by saying, for example, "I am thankful and delighted that the new car I want is already mine." Always write in the present tense, and the universe will deliver.

Actively and Audibly Ask the Universe for It

Once you know what you want and have it down on paper, ask for it. There are many ways that people address this step of the Law of Attraction, but I believe that prayers are the most common way of asking. You can ask at any time; you do not have to shout it out, but say it loud enough for the universe to hear you.

Let the universe know what you want, how you want it, in what quantity, and such—and while requesting what you want, believe it is yours and see it as yours. You can only be given what you ask for.

Trust the Universe and Believe That You Will Get It

Once you have asked for what you want, move on to believing and trusting that you have got what you want.

Stop worrying about what you asked for and how you will get it—leave the "how" to the universe and concentrate on the core principles of belief, trust, and appreciation. Do not run around in your mind anticipating or seeking what you asked for and do not rush. Be patient and do not lose hope or be upset if things do not start happening immediately. Some asks have taken decades to be answered; everything in nature happens in its own time.

You should move on in your stride and let the universe do the worrying on your behalf.

Meditation and Visualization

Mental relaxation is by far the easiest and surest way to get mental serenity and clarity, the precursors to attaining the right frame of mind for success.

You need to take up one of the many forms of meditation that can easily fit into your lifestyle and that you are comfortable practicing. It is needful for you to keep in mind that not everybody can do any form of meditation, due to age, health conditions, size, etc.

For optimal mind relaxation and rejuvenation, it is recommended to perform guided meditations for five to ten minutes at a time, in a setting that is quiet and devoid of distractions. Early morning or late night meditations are appropriate because these are the times where your surroundings are likely to be serene.

Once your mind is serene and clear, you can move on to active visualization; create exact mental images of what you want, and visualize them every time you go into a guided meditation. If you imagine something long enough, it will manifest faster.

Pick your object of desire, choose it in your mind with exact details, for example, a green 4 door Peugeot; visualize it every day and meditate upon it until the day the universe delivers it to you.

Own and Possess

Once you have asked for the job promotion or the new house you desire, you need to put yourself in a state of mind where you feel like you already have it.

This step is what we commonly refer to as faith; absolute belief in the abstract is required, which is difficult but possible if you train your mind to lead you there. This is the most important of all the action steps you will read here, yet it is also the most elusive.

Smile even if you are not happy, and your spirit will inevitably be lifted, and you will feel better; use the same principle for all the bigger things you want, and they will come to you.

The law starts working here, so you must own and possess what is yours in your mind before it manifests itself in reality.

Gratitude — Be Thankful for Everything in Your Life

Gratitude is a key ingredient for success using the principles of the Law of Attraction. Be grateful for what you had, for what you have, for what you are asking for, and for what you are going to have. You must be forever grateful for the blessings in your life, whether material or immaterial.

Jot write down the things you are grateful for and always remember to thank the universe for them; just like you and I are motivated when someone shows gratitude for what you have done for them, it is the same in the laws of nature.

Basically, the Law of Attraction is heightened when you appreciate what it gives you.

Think About It More and Think Positively

This is not a contradiction of what we discussed earlier, contrary to worrying; positive thoughts about what you want is greatly profitable to you. What you think about most is what you attract and what you become; therefore, what better things to think about than positive things you have asked the universe for?

Stop thinking about what you do not desire or allow yourself to be bothered by the negative happenings of the past; negativity will simply cause more negativity.

Your thoughts cause your feelings and your feelings attract. Having positive inner thoughts and happy outer feelings is important for success; a positive mindset is seldom stuck in the gloom. Your thoughts control your feelings, and that is why it is important to cultivate and nurture feel-good thoughts and emotions for an upbeat attitude.

Mahatma Gandhi said that what you believe becomes what you think. Your thoughts are your words, your words then become your actions, your actions turn to your habits, your habits become your values, and your values are your destiny.

Be happy, feel excited about life, be passionate about things, laugh, smile, and the world will give you the same emotions right back.

Begin to Talk About What You Want

Talk about what you want and what you 'have already got' with others and include them in your dreams. I would recommend sharing this with positive people because they will help encourage you to remain on the right path and remind you of the goal in case you stray off.

Speak in undeterred knowledge and belief that what you want is a package in the courier on the way to you.

Act Towards What You Want

You might have heard the famous saying, "Faith without action is dead," and there is no better place the truism applies than in the endeavor to succeed.

If you do not work for success, you cannot be successful; it is as simple as that. Do not expect that deciding what you want, writing it down, and simply reclining in a shell and not doing anything is going to get you there. NO WAY.

There is no luck in getting what you want—even those who win lotteries or any other contests do work to get it. Yes, they buy the tickets or take the time to register for the draws. Success is not a miracle, the right mindset is not a miracle, and the Law of Attraction is certainly not miraculous.

These steps in mastering the Law of Attraction will surely get you to the right mindset for success in your life. These principles can only work for you if you make them part of your daily life and routine; you must use them daily, just like how you have to drink and eat every day.

Success is achieved by habit; make these principles your habits to help you achieve the right mindset for success.

Success Stories of Famous People Using the Law of Attraction

Oprah Winfrey

Oprah Winfrey is a celebrity who believes in and has propagated the adoption of the law for a better and successful life. She has used her TV show to promote the law, invited host writers and teachers of the principle, and she recommends books on the subject.

She has cited how the Law of Attraction helped her land a role in the movie 'The Color Purple' by constantly attracting the role to her through sustained and purposed thought and mental imagery to be in the movie if it was ever made.

From the time Oprah read the book, she says she felt attached to it and knew that one day it would be a movie; she immediately started preparing for the role before the movie ever came to fruition or even before she was called to an audition.

She claims that the Law of Attraction has worked for her to great success, not just to land the role in the movie but also in other spheres of her life, especially her media career. In fact, Oprah Winfrey admits that she did not know about the law initially - she was practicing it unconsciously and came to realize she was a practitioner later on when she learned of it and realized that her way of thinking adheres to the exact same principles like the Law of Attraction.

Jim Carrey

Jim Carrey, a very successful actor in his own right, is a manifestation of the Law of Attraction. He is a great believer in the ability of our thoughts to create who we are.

From humble beginnings in the mid-1980s when he could not get a job despite film directors praising him for how good his work was, Jim Carrey grew to be one of the highest-paid and grossing Hollywood actors today.

He believed and practiced the art and techniques of mental visualization of himself and circumstances to where and whom he wanted to be, and channeled and controlled his thoughts in the direction of his desires until he got his first million-dollar paycheck.

Jim Carrey wrote himself a $10-million-dollar paycheck and carried it around in his wallet for years before he made the actual amount for a movie that propelled him to phenomenal success in 1995, about 10 years after he wrote the dummy check.

He practiced daily visualization and controlled his mindset to help him with the career success that he desired; he actively channeled his thoughts for his success to the point that the world around him made the success that he so voraciously desired work for him.

The actor has an unwavering belief in the power of intention and mental visualization in realizing and mastering the law.

Effect of the Law of Attraction When Mingling with Positive and Negative People

The general idea is that thoughts are attractive and they convey intentions; in effect, the law states that you can be around negative people and not be influenced or swayed at all by their negativity, while you can be around positive people and grow from it.

Why?

Well, it is just because you hold power! It is not those around you who decide what you think or attract; it is you. The power of attraction is within you, controlled by you, and decided by you. So, to put it simply, all you need to learn is how to cope with negative people so that they have no undesired influence in the direction of your thoughts.

Interestingly, most negativity tends to come from those closest to us for various reasons; they may not believe in our dreams, they do not understand our newly acquired way of life, or they are simply pessimist and cynical.

For the Law of Attraction to work for you and to get you attracting all the success, you have to choose to be around the right people in order for you to get to the correct mindset. Be with people who are positive, who can encourage you and help make you a better person.

Keep people with negative vibes at arm's length or help them get in the same mindset as you.

Here are some things you can do to help negative people around you turn around:

- Get them to tell you or talk about what they want instead of what they do not want. That will usually get them to stop complaining and concentrate on the positive; it will shift the negative energy into a reservoir of positive attraction.

- When dealing with a negative person, put on a mental shield to prepare you to deal with the unwanted vibe. Approach your meeting with a positive attitude and take control of it by directing it in a healthy direction.

- Talk to the person and explain to them the Law of Attraction and tell them that you are living by it. Most people will not be aware that they are hurting your plans until you tell them, and when you do, they will most likely be sensitive to your wishes and will even encourage you.

- If it does not work, then it is time to let them go or meet them only on rare occasions.

By surrounding yourself with like-minded people, you get uplifted and enhance the intensity of the positive energy around you—discard negative people, or control your encounters to enhance positive energy.

Harnessing your energy on the negativity of people will only get you more negative people and negativity around you because that is what you are attracting. Shift your focus to the positive aspects of these people and situations to enhance your success through the Law of Attraction.

The Power of the Subconscious Mind or Mental Blueprints

"To unleash your hidden potential, you have to tap into your subconscious mind power" — Tony Robbins

If personal change does not first take place on the subconscious level, it will never happen. Changing the way that we think is the key to changing our lives and getting what we want or desire. Working the subconscious to create a change of mindset is as simple as planting the idea of what you want in your mind and intensely concentrating on it over a period of time.

By working on the subconscious, you are likely to release the power of your subconscious mind and come up with ways to get what you want within the time you gave yourself. In the Law of Attraction, you are supposed to attract things, not run after them, and the subconscious mind is the key to get it to work.

Most of us fall short because we may have an intense desire to succeed but fail to give specific instructions regarding what we want to the subconscious mind; without your inner mind not knowing what you want, you cannot possibly get the wheels turning to achieve it.

So, how do we tune in and awaken the subconscious mind to what we want?

Create a Vision Board

Have a pictorial version of your goal and hang it somewhere that you see every day; this helps your subconscious mind pick up on and start vibrating out your dream to the universe.

Write Down Your Goals Right Before You Sleep Every Night

There is no better and proven method of influencing your subconscious than by triggering or stimulating it just before you go to bed.

Your brain is most active when as you sleep. By writing your goals down every night before you sleep, you will saturate your mind with the thoughts and ideas of your goals, making it aware and aligning it with what you want.

How Does the Subconscious Mind Work?

The subconscious mind is full of much more power than you can imagine, and it works for us in more ways than we even realize; it is the engine that keeps our body running; it is the nerve center for memory; it controls our muscles and makes us function with ease.

If you think about it, everything you do is controlled by your inner mind; it learns and masters everything we do, then takes over the job. Now, imagine what it can do for you in changing your mindset, attracting what you want, and giving you success.

How Does the Law of Attraction Collaborate with Your Subconscious Mind for Success?

As you now know, the law of attraction is simple; what you think about most is what you get, and it happens because you are either knowingly or unknowingly instructing it to your subconscious mind.

The subconscious mind is very powerful, and we should, therefore, know how to harvest and use its power to our advantage and success.

Think positively to instruct your subconscious to relay positive vibes, which, in turn, attract success. You must give your subconscious instructions, and it will learn how to help you.

Your subconscious mind learns by repeating; the more you do something, the better you become because your inner mind begins to help you with memorization, actions, and reactions. Not only can the subconscious know what we want from memory, but we can tell it what we desire through repeated vocalization or thought.

Decide what you want, tell yourself over and over, and your subconscious will start working on getting you to your goal.

Common Mistakes to Avoid!

The Law of Attraction does not work for most people because there is a disconnect in their understanding of setting goals and achieving them. Setting your goals is an imaginative yet rational process while realizing the goals you have set involves feelings or emotions and habits. You must understand what it means to set goals and achieve them.

The other problem is that people actually get to the point of adopting positive thoughts but do not realize the desired positive results because of contradictory subconscious vibrations. If you remember what we learned earlier about the subconscious, you know that if your inner mind does not correspond to your desires, then everything you do is questionable. Your attraction is generated and determined by the subconscious mind.

Having a vision and a dream is good, but you must get your conscious mind and the more powerful and influential subconscious mind to be on the same page—with synchronicity, which is only achievable through repetitive indoctrination. You have to turn your desires into emotions and impress it on the subconscious, even as you take action towards achieving your goals.

If you want things to happen for you, just saying what you want is not enough. You must truly believe and trust that you are going to get it. Visualize what you want and believe that you will get it, without even the slightest doubt. Whenever you have doubts, alter your thought pattern to a positive one.

Avoid negative terms that will only attract negative results; if you want to get out of debt, for example, talk about having money. Avoid conversations with the word debt in them because the more you talk about it, the more debt you will be attracting—and the more you talk about having money, the more money you will attract.

Having the right mindset will determine if you are going to succeed or fail.

We have learned what it entails to get to the right mindset through the simple but incredibly powerful concept of the Law of Attraction. By applying positive mind-altering ideas, you will be able to attract whatever you want to your life for a successful, wholesome, and healthy life.

You now know beyond a doubt that your thoughts manifest into habits, so it is up to you to decide what kind of thoughts you want in your mind. If you want to achieve success, do choose and work for positive thoughts—and if you want a gloomy life, you can settle for negativity.

I wish you a positive life, and I hope you attract all the success you wish for. The next step is to adopt the techniques we discussed and use them to attain the success that awaits you.

Chapter 7: Relaxation

If you are going to hack your mindset, you need to know how to move between the states of focus and relaxation. After all, a happy mind is a sharp mind and one that's getting a little rest between periods of being active and sharp.

Ways to Relax

With that being said, what are the best techniques for this? We've collected a number of ways that you can relax at home or simply make the most of your personal lunch or 15-minute work breaks. Check them out, see which ones do appeal to you most, and give them a try!

1. Add Some Distraction to Your Break Routine

A good way to reboot your mind state is with the use of distraction; do something completely out of the norm for your daily routine. The reasoning behind how this hacks your mindset is that our brains tend to skip over details from a number of events that have become routine. It makes sense. You don't need to remember every car you see on your daily commute, and if you've got a particular favorite breakfast, you are only going to notice if the cook changes the recipe or if one day it is particularly bland or really good. We mostly notice changes from the norm. So, spice things up a bit. Eat with someone you've never eaten with on your lunch break. Occasionally pack lunch and eat outside. Changes in your routine can help reboot your mindset and enable you to be more focused for the rest of the day.

2. Exercise

Surprisingly enough, taking a jog or running on your lunch break can invigorate you for the rest of the day. It releases endorphins that can stabilize your mood and energize you in preparation for the rest of your day. Carry extra clothes to change in your car if it's warm out, but a quick run shouldn't require a wardrobe change. Hack your way to an endorphin edge with a little exercise on your breaks!

3. Call a Friend

One way to invigorate yourself and to help make sure you are staying social is to just give a friend a call on a break. Socializing is good for us and can improve our morale for the rest of the day. Also, when you are home, a quick call to a friend can improve your mood and help keep you social and centered. Consider this social-friendly Mindset Hack to give you a little refreshing escape and subsequent edge for your busy workday!

4. Meditate

We've dedicated an entire chapter on methods that you can use (Chapter 8, if you have been skipping around). Meditation isn't just for gurus or Buddhist priests. Clearing your mind and taking a moment to enjoy the world around you can keep you relaxed and boost your creativity. Used daily, it can also greatly contribute to self-control. Give it a try and see what it can do for you!

5. Read a Good Book

It seems old-fashioned, but we have included this here because it truly works, and has for some time. A book takes you into an immersive experience that you can carry with you anywhere. Try to read a little every day on breaks, and you'll be surprised at the productivity boost that this little distraction can provide. This time-and-tested mindset hack is sure never to fail.

6. Creative Writing

Creative writing is a good way to express yourself while separating your mind from your work for some time. You can write about anything that you like, and you will find that the minutes just fly. Applying yourself creatively in this fashion can help you build your imagination so that you can better 'think outside of the box.' Give it a try sometime!

7. Bread for Serotonin

Did you know that things like whole grain bread, rice, and oatmeal can help your body produce a mood-boosting chemical called serotonin? Well, now you know, and you should take advantage of it. Pack one of these three for your breaks and give yourself a mindset-hacking mood boost!

8. Surprise Beverages

This one is fun, effective, and refreshing. When you are shopping, get single-serving sized bottles or cans of various beverages. When you get home, take some plastic bags and put them in 2's or 3's, in different combinations, into opaque plastic bags that you will tie and put in the refrigerator. In the morning, when you leave for work, grab a bag and take it with you. When you go on a break or just need a pick-me-up, get a cup of ice and without peeking, pull a drink out of the bag. The variety gives you a quick mini-distraction so that you can reap the benefits of a little change of routine with very little effort.

9. Weekend in Bed

Treat yourself to the occasional 'weekend in bed' where you order out and watch movies in bed. Some people believe that in order to really enjoy yourself on the weekends you have to go out and socialize all the time, but this is simply not true. Taking some time for yourself is good for you, and you won't believe how relaxed you feel when you go to work on Monday. Order a pizza, watch some movies, and if you can, don't leave that bed. Sometimes, the simplest pleasures are the best!

10. Bucket List

Get a piece of paper and make a list of things that you can do on the weekend, preferably things that you would like to do but have never done before. Ensure that you leave ample space between each item for what comes next. Cut each item into strips and fold them so that you cannot see what they say. Next, put them in a bowl that you keep somewhere handy (or for extra points, an actual bucket where you've written 'Bucket List Bucket' on the side) and when you get out of work on Friday, go home, reach into the bucket, and pull one out.

Do whatever you have listed on the selected strip of paper. This is yet another method to add a little something to your rest and relaxation time. It forces a change of routine that will help make sure that you arrive to work on Monday energized, sharp, and possibly with a new hobby.

Besides, it's a lot of fun!

11. Leave Work at Work

You would never bring your personal problems into your workspace, so practice the opposite and leave your work issues at work. When you get out of the office, all of your time and focus should be on you. Allowing yourself to bring your work-persona into your home will take a lot of the fun out of your weekends, a time where you should be resting and enjoying yourself. As a result, you'll perform less adeptly the following week. The effect is cumulative, so you need to put a stop to it immediately. To get the most out of your relaxation time, keep your two lives separate. Trust me; you'll be glad that you did.

12. Make a Monster Breakfast

Throughout the workweek, your breakfast is probably not as stellar as you might like. A quick McMuffin or breakfast burrito, possibly a cup of yogurt and an apple. But it's the weekend now, so you should indulge yourself. Why not treat yourself to a monster breakfast? Whip up some pancakes. Throw some bread in the toaster to have with the jam of your choice. Fry some bacon and make some sunny side up eggs in the bacon grease. Add some hash browns or a little oatmeal on the side and indulge yourself. As an added bonus, you are likely to have plenty of leftovers that you can snack on all day. Even better, invite a friend to share it with. Treating yourself every now and again will help keep you in a relaxed mindset so that you can maximize the restful nature of the weekend. You deserve it.

13. Spend Some Time in Nature

Camping on your day off, hiking, or simply spending a little time watching the birds in your local park or arboretum can be good for the soul and excellent for a healthy, relaxed mindset. Pack a lunch to bring with you along with a good book and find somewhere secluded and beautiful to spend a little time in nature. We have routines at home that consume more time than we realize, and this can make our time off seem really short. When you are in nature, however, minutes can feel like glorious hours. Take advantage of this. It's free, and it's good for you. How long has it been since you spent a little time in nature? Well, get out there, because it's been too long!

14. Feed Your Hobbies

Do you have a hobby that really gets your juices flowing? Why not turn off your smartphone, get into your workshop or home office, and invest a little time in it. Do some creative writing. Enjoy a do-it-yourself project that will give you something practical to use in the house. Paint a picture or make a sculpture. Scrapbook some memories, if that's your thing. Everyone has hobbies, but it can be difficult to make time for them if you don't allow yourself to embrace the proper mindset. So, enough waiting—feed that hobby of yours and refresh yourself through the power of creative expression. There's really nothing else quite like it, so don't neglect your hobbies. They are the Mindset Hacks that you never knew you had!

15. Knock Out Chores During the Week

This little piece of advice is both practical and wonderful. Knock out your chores during the week so that you don't have to deal with them on the weekend. This will free you up for leisure or fun and also helps to compartmentalize your work time against your leisure time. Letting chores pile up until the weekend is a mistake that is easy to make if you don't plan ahead, so make a list if you need and post it on the refrigerator as a reminder. Make your weekends your own with this little tip to enjoy them to the fullest. If you simply don't have the time to do this, you can occasionally hire someone to clean on Friday while you are working, but if possible, simply knocking them out incrementally through the week is the way to go. Free up your time and own those weekends; you deserve a break!

16. Weekend Trip

You might not know this, but some travel agencies can provide you with a weekend trip to a completely random location. This is a bit of an adventure. You get to go somewhere you might not have visited before, meet new and interesting people, and relax while enjoying local foods. Of course, your trip doesn't have to be random, and it also doesn't even have to be far. A trip to a neighboring city for a weekend of R and R can sometimes be just what you need to break your routine and properly unwind. Give this a try and enjoy yourself a little on your free time.

17. Go for a Bike Ride

Most of us spent countless hours of our childhoods gliding across the sidewalks and practically flying down hills on our favorite mode of transportation—the good ol' bicycle. If you haven't ridden one in years, you should consider renting or investing in one so that you can recapture a bit of the nostalgia. You never forget how to ride a bike, and gliding through the park can take you straight back to childhood glee, with the wind in your face as the trees pass by. Little mind hacks like this can go a long way in boosting your morale and putting you into high spirits. What are you waiting for? It's time to take a ride!

18. Create a Traditional 'Weekend Herald'

A nice way to put yourself into 'weekend mode' is to create some sort of ritual for when you first get home. It can be a particular song that you play every time you start the weekend, a bell that you ring joyously, or my personal favorite, a gong that you whack right after entering the domicile. This is symbolic, and on a subconscious level, it hacks your mindset into recreation and relaxation mode. You'll just have to try it to see, but as silly as it sounds, this is both fun and effective.

19. Silence the Cellphone

If you have already made plans, keep your smartphone on silent. If there is someone that you need to communicate with because you are meeting with them, text them to tell them that you will be checking the phone infrequently and that after you meet, you intend to be incommunicado for the rest of the weekend. Spending too much time on your smartphone can make your weekends feel small, as you really do not realize just how much time those wonderful little gadgets can waste. Tune out a little and silence your smartphone so that you can enjoy your weekend. The phone will still be there for you on Monday.

20. Try a New Food with a Friend

Make a weekend ritual with your best friend or significant other, where you will both try a new food or restaurant once every weekend. This is fun and relaxing because it breaks the routine while satiating the desire to be social by enjoying a new, shared experience. Also, you never know, you might find discover amazing new foods that were just around the corner this whole time. Why not go out this weekend and explore the culinary world?

Ready to get the most out of your free time? We're happy to hear that. We hope that you will use these tips and tricks to make the most of that precious you-time. After all the work you do, don't you think you deserve it?

Stress

So, what is stress?

Stress is basically the body's way of responding to pressure that may be exerted on it physically or psychologically. Stress is caused when the body releases stress chemicals, usually adrenaline into the blood in an effort to combat whatever pressure it is confronted with.

Stress can be classified as follows:

- Survival stress - this is the stress we face when we are confronted by dangerous situations, and when we feel that physical harm is imminent. This is where we have a fight and flight response to fight against stress.

- Internal stress - this is stress caused by worries over things that are out of your control. Simply put, internal stress is self-imposed stress that can be avoided by not putting yourself under too much pressure over things that are beyond you.

- Environmental stress - this is stress caused by factors in your surroundings like noise etc. Stay away from environmental stress triggers to lead a happy life.

- Tiredness - this type of stress is caused by fatigue, which usually accumulates over a long period of time due to overworking.

Stress is an inescapable part of life, and sooner or later, we experience it. What we need to do is learn how to manage it so that it does not overwhelm us and take over our lives.

Stress is not an entirely bad thing as it can enhance our alertness and concentration; however, in excess, it is extremely unhealthy.

Symptoms of Stress

How do you know if you are stressed?

The following are signs that will let you know if you are stressed:

Cognitive Symptoms

- Problems remembering things

- Low concentration

- High anxiety

- Constant worry

Emotional Symptoms

- Being moody

- Highly irritable and angry

- Loneliness and reclusion

- Sadness

Physical Symptoms

- Low libido

- Aches and pain

- High heart rate

- Dizziness

Behavioral Symptoms

- Eating disorders - bingeing or self-starving

- Lack of sleep

- Substance abuse

- Nervousness

Causes of Stress

External Causes

- Major life changes; divorce, chronic illness, the death of a loved one

- Work burden

- Financial problems

- Trauma

Internal Causes

- Constant worry

- Negativity and pessimism

- Fear and anxiety

- Unrealistic expectations

If not dealt with immediately, stress can cause serious health and social problems. Some of the side effects of stress include:

- Mental disorders like depression and anxiety

- Cardiovascular problems; high blood pressure, heart disease, stroke, etc.

- Weight problems such as obesity

- Problems with menstrual cycles

- Skin and hair problems; acne, hair loss, etc.

- Sexual dysfunction

- Gastrointestinal problems such as ulcers

Meditation and Stress Management

Meditation has been proven to be a stress reliever and is embraced by many for its relaxation. Stress relief needs both mental and physical relaxation, and meditation provides just that.

To understand why meditation is so helpful in reducing stress, you need to know what it takes to relax:

Deep Breathing

Deep breathing is a quick and sure way of deflating stress from your system; it is a simple technique with far-reaching positive consequences in keeping stress in check.

Balancing the Nervous System

For the body to function optimally, the nervous system must be at equilibrium - you must be at peace mentally. Stress destabilizes this balance, and the only way to steady your system is by relaxing and getting into a state of profound serenity, which is counter to stress.

Yoga

Yoga is a series of steady movements and stationary poses combined with deep breathing.

If practiced regularly, yoga reduces stress and improves flexibility, strength, balance, and stamina.

Almost all types of yoga are beneficial for stress relief as they combine steady movement, deep breathing, and stretching. You may try the following types:

Satyananda

This is a traditional form of Yoga that uses meditation, gentle poses, and deep relaxation—and it is ideal for those who want to start practicing yoga for stress relief.

Hatha Yoga

This is also a gentle form of yoga that is ideal for you to ease your way into the practice.

Power Yoga

Power Yoga is more advanced and is for those who are already familiar with the basics of yoga. It is more intense, and the focus is on fitness, so it is ideal for those seeking relaxation and stimulation.

Tai Chi

Tai Chi is a mellow form of meditation suited for everyone. It is especially good for the elderly recovering from injuries and to treat illnesses common with those of advanced age.

It is a series of slow body movements emphasizing concentration, circulation of energy through the body, and relaxation while focusing on breathing.

For you to effectively deal with stress through meditation, it is important to be consistent in practicing whichever type of meditation you settle for. Make it part of your life and practice it regularly until it becomes second nature.

What you need to do for a successful stress-relieving meditation experience:

- Get a quiet, serene place for your meditation exercise; this can be anywhere as long as you are not bothered. It can be in your backyard, living room, in a park, etc.

- Assume a comfortable posture, whether seated, standing, or lying down. Start tuning your mind to the "now" — focus and concentrate.

- In the posture with eyes closed, take a slow deep breath and relax your body as you do this. Get into a rhythm of inhaling and exhaling.

- Clear your mind of distracting thoughts and concentrate on your meditation. Pay attention to your breathing and concentrate only on that as you relax.

- Channel your mind to thoughts of a happy place you have been to, or simply concentrate on the present while listening to your breathing. Push out unwanted thoughts that may come your way.

- Keep your eyes closed, take deep breaths, and imagine your body relaxing. Keep doing this until you are completely relaxed.

Imagine a life of reduced stress; isn't that what we all want? By following the advice and tips discussed above, you will be able to effectively kick out stress from your life and remain a happy and relaxed individual.

Depression

Whenever stress gets out of control, depression sets in. Depression is a condition that is directly linked to the mismanagement of stress.

Depression is the disorder of a person's mood or emotions, causing sadness and loss of interest.

When one is faced with extreme emotions or feelings of hopelessness, sadness, despair, or low self-esteem, they can be considered depressed. This type of depression is situational as it is triggered by circumstances that the person is dealing with.

Clinically, depression is caused by a chemical imbalance in the brain, causing bipolar disorder and manic depression, which are generally referred to as an organic depression. Stress hormones (cortisol and epinephrine) found in adrenaline have proven to be responsible for organic depression.

Symptoms of Depression

Depression is usually exhibited or accompanied by the following symptoms:

- Loss of interest in hobbies and usual activities

- Reclusiveness

- Feelings of hopelessness and worthlessness

- Difficulty or lack of sleep

- Restlessness and fatigue

- Lower concentration

- Suicidal thoughts

Once in a while, we all face some form of mild depression. Unfortunately, some of us experience extreme forms of this condition that can overwhelm us, leading to significant mental deterioration, social self-exclusion, and even suicide, in some cases.

Causes of Depression

Depression is caused by a number of factors or, in some instances, a combination of the following factors:

- Encounters with stressful events, such as the death of a loved one or the breakdown of a relationship, which can lead to a serious emotional turmoil that may lead to depression

- Chronic and long-term illness

- Some personality traits are more vulnerable to depression, such as low self-esteem, etc.

- Family history - those from families where some have suffered depression before are highly likely to be affected

- Giving birth - some women get postnatal depression because of physical and emotional changes

- Loneliness and drug abuse

- Chemical changes in the brain - clinical depression

- Physical and emotional abuse

- Some medication

- Conflicts

The good news is that depression can significantly be managed and even treated through meditation.

Conclusion

If you are always late and short of time, then you are most likely leading a stressed life; there is nothing as stressful as the struggle to always meet a deadline or catch up with something you forgot about. Using the little time that we have in a proper manner will help you cope with stress.

Time management involves methods aimed at using time efficiently to perform all the tasks we have within a given time and involves prioritizing, scheduling, and organizing.

You must assess the tasks on your plate and put them in order of importance and urgency to avoid confusion, conflicts, and unnecessary time pressures.

Plan things in advance to avoid last-minute scrambling in an effort to get something that skipped your mind done.

Good time management makes you a more productive person; you will do more within a short time, thus gaining more control of your life.

Create a schedule and stick to it; you will have enough free time to engage in fun things that you have been missing. You will have time to go to the movies, play a game, or any other fun activity which serves to boost health and well-being.

Good time management means that you have enough time for work, family, and friends. These moments with loved ones are the most fulfilling and stress-relieving.

It does not take much to be a good time manager; all you need is start and commit to it. Well-managed time leads to a more comfortable and happy life.

The benefits of time management for a less stressful life are:

- Doing more with less time

- Getting more free time, which allows time to relax

- Stress is reduced since you do not worry about pending deadlines, etc.

- Higher productivity - you are fresh, mentally/physically prepared, and highly motivated.

Time management is good because you will be happier, more successful, more productive, and more capable of living a fuller and stress-free life. Why don't you start managing your time better and enjoy the benefits?

Thanks again for downloading this book!

I hope this book was able to help you bring order to your life and get rid of procrastination.

The next step is to continue practicing what you have learned here and to make it a part of your everyday life. I advise you to continue improving your organizational skills by doing more research on how to avoid procrastination.

Finally, if you enjoyed this book, would you be kind enough to leave a review for it on Amazon? It'd be greatly appreciated!